IMPROV LEADERSHIP

A Comedian's Guide To Effective Leadership In An Unscripted Workplace

ANDREW BRIGHT

Improv Leadership

Copyright © 2017 by Andrew Bright

ISBN: 9780692887424

Edited by: Kimberlyn Bridges
Cover Design: Kimberlyn Bridges/Andrew Bright
Photography: Stock photography
Author Photographs: Dann Warick

To my wife, Karla.

I said, "I'm thinking of writing a book."

You said, "You should do it. It will be great."

I believed you.

iv

Table Of Contents

Introduction

We All Do Improv

"That was incredible! I could never do what you do."

I've heard it a hundred times following a great improv performance. Audience members in awe of the spontaneous scenes, rich characters and hilarious comedy that is part of an excellent improv show.

Sure, we all have things that come naturally to us and things that don't. I love being on stage, but don't ask me to fix your computer. If you want your computer fixed, take it to the vet.

The thing is, you probably do improv more than you realize. Life is unscripted. People are unpredictable. Unexpected change is a part of our lives.

Learning to operate effectively within the unknown is an essential skill is our fast-paced, ever changing world. Improv is less about what decision to make next, and more about how to make decisions. The better you become at learning to operate in any situation the less the situation itself matters.

That's how improv works. Improv comedy is amazing. There is no script and no director. You don't hold a meeting before starting the scene or vote on ideas before picking one. You simply go, now. Listening is key, trust and respect are paramount and forward momentum is everything.

The key factor in whether you fly or flop depends less on how funny you are as an individual and more on how well you work as a team. In improv, teamwork trumps individual talent all day long. Leadership is key, too. You have to know when to lead and when to follow. Both are essential.

You can learn a lot from improv. As much as we'd like it to, life doesn't follow a script. Change is constant. The most rewarding and important work is often done in unknown territory. That's why people who do new things are called Pioneers.

What if you were comfortable in unknown territory? What could be possible? What if you became a leader who others love to follow? What could your team accomplish together?

Twenty years of performing professional improv comedy has made me a better leader, husband, father and friend. I can't wait to pass on what I've learned to you. My guess is you are already doing improv. I want to show you how to do it well.

My focus for this book is leadership through the lens of improv comedy. I love leadership. Great leaders inspire others, push the envelope and change the world. Improv has so much to say on leadership. In this book we'll take a look at the following important topics:

Leading in Circles - Improv's recipe for effective, empowering leadership. Learn how to follow as well as you lead and support your team in ways that relate to their needs and help them grow. Bring momentum to your leadership.

Perception - How you view your organization, your team and your role as a leader affects your ability to lead well. I'll break down what makes an improv scene work and teach you to push through fear and ego, form a correct perspective and create great things with your team.

Direction and Structure - The most creative people use structure to enhance their ability to create. Structure equals freedom. Learn the best ways to bring direction and structure to your team.

Creating a Culture of Celebration - We win more often that we think. Discover how creating a culture of celebration will motivate your team to push harder and accomplish more.

Amazing Performance or Perform Amazingly - Too often we focus more on serving our customer than serving our team. I'll show you 5 ways to care for your team so they consistently perform amazingly.

The Secret Sauce – How to Really Win in Improv and Leadership - It's the reason audiences love improv so much and it's an opportunity to become an incredible leader who resonates with your team. Learn the power of being authentic and vulnerable with the people you lead.

Ready? Let's go.

6 Introduction

Chapter 1: Leading in Circles

The best way to lead in improv comedy is a principle I call "Leading in Circles." It's a horrible idea if you're lost in the woods, but invaluable in running your team or organization. In improv there is no boss. No supervisor of the scene. No manager of material. We all simply lead and follow at the same time, in the moment. Imagine effectively leading while following and supporting your team, who, in turn, become leaders as they follow you. **Leading in circles.**

Novice actors struggle to know when to lead and when to follow. They tend to push their ideas relentlessly or follow faithfully but never voice their own great offers. When an actor learns to lead and follow, directing and supporting in the moment, it's a beautiful thing.

I believe some leaders mistake driving for leading. They like to drive their team forward. Carry the water. Take it to the next level. First one on the field, last one to leave. Insert your own inspirational cliché here.

I don't deny the merit of leading from the front. It is important to lead by example. It is essential for your team to know you are passionate and committed.

I also believe that many leaders are missing a powerful leadership opportunity when they neglect to allow themselves to be led. Asking your team for help and being willing to follow another's lead is an incredibly affirming and effective act of leadership.

Unfortunately, many leaders, myself included, struggle with this.

Lonely Leadership

Call it what you want—self-reliance, independence, fear, pride. However you define it, I suffer from it. I struggle with the mentality that says, "If you want something done right...refuse to let anyone help you." That's not the popular ending you expected, but it's the truth, isn't it?

Acting alone, no matter how noble the intent, is an act of excluding others. Allowing yourself to rely on others, however, is a powerful way to strengthen a relationship and feed another's growth as a leader. Asking for help is freeing for you, empowering to your team and great for relationships.

Organizational health guru Patrick Lencioni wrote a blog post back in 2011 that shifted the way I view seeking help from others. In it he states,

"People actually feel better about themselves and about someone else when they are in the position of

being a helper, rather than a helpee. That's because helpers receive a sense of contribution and confidence, while helpees often feel dependent and in debt to someone."[1]

There's a simple way to test this theory. How do you feel when someone asks you for help? I don't mean when your old college roommate asks you to help him move for the third time. Nor do I mean when your boyfriend's second cousin asks you to co-sign for a loan.

I mean when someone truly wants your advice or assistance because they value what you have to offer. How does it make you feel? Now contrast this with the way you feel when you consider asking someone else to help you. Is there a difference?

I am someone who is energized by helping others. If you ask me for help, I relish the chance to be of service and will often put your project ahead of my own. That's part of my people-pleasing nature. I feel valued and confident when someone needs me, yet I struggle to ask others for help.

I receive a genuine lift in spirit, a boost in confidence and sense of achievement when I have the opportunity to assist someone else, yet I refuse to offer that same sense of value and accomplishment to another because I don't want to put them out. Anyone else see the irony in this perspective?

Lencioni reports that when he began to ask his team for help in areas in which he genuinely admired their ability, he saw and felt the difference. He states,

"I am convinced that I have built much stronger relationships with each of these people, and contributed to their sense of confidence and importance, by genuinely expressing my admiration for them and asking for their assistance. All that I have done is acknowledged – and rightly so – their superiority to me in various, important areas, and made myself vulnerable to them. This has not diminished my authority as their leader at work, but rather made it abundantly clear that they have as

much to offer me as I do them, in spite of the hierarchy at work."[2]

Asking your team for help is not weakness, it's leadership. It's the strength to see you are not capable of doing something as well as someone else on your team. It's the humility to ask for help. It's the awareness to offer your team an opportunity to grow through leading you.

Sowing Leadership Into Others

Do you know how I get hesitant, rookie actors to lead? I ask for their ideas. On stage in the middle of the performance and in character, of course, I'll ask, "What's next?" Then I wait. Even if it becomes a bit awkward, I wait. When they offer up an idea, no matter if it's incredible or mediocre, I support it with everything I have, and the whole team builds on it. You should see the look of pride and confidence that breaks across that actor's face! It's priceless.

Here's the best part. As an improv actor gains more confidence and experience, they not only begin contributing more ideas, they work harder to support others. They have experienced firsthand the power of feeling valued and supported. As they learn to lead, they graciously offer that same opportunity to the rest of the team.

Let's Get Physical

Leading in circles means sometimes you are leading and sometimes you are following. What determines whether you lead or follow is not your role in the company or your level of experience. The determining factor is what's needed to move forward in that moment.

A big part of knowing when to lead and when to follow is knowing your team. We all have areas we thrive in and those we struggle through. We all have different passions and abilities. I'm a horrible singer. It took a while for my mother to realize this because she is very good at seeing the good in others, even if it's not really that good.

My family is musical. My parents can both sing and play the piano. My brother can sing and play several instruments. My sister can sing, too. I may have been adopted.

We used to sit around the piano and sing together as a family, a time I fondly refer to as house arrest. One particular evening it was my turn to sing a solo. The song was, "He's Still Working on Me" by Bill and Gloria Gaither. How appropriate.

I was giving it my best shot, but my mother was getting frustrated. She would stop playing, turn to me and say, "Andrew, quit goofing off. Try your best." To her credit, I was prone to goofing off, but I wasn't this time.

Finally, I remember my father gently placing his hands on my mother's shoulders and saying, "Lois, I believe he IS trying his best." My mother looked at me with wide eyes and didn't say another word. Thankfully, that marked the end of my house arrest solo career.

My family also played charades, and I CRUSHED it! I had a knack for physical comedy, and I could act out anything. When my mother would read Bible stories to us in the evening, she would allow me to silently act out the story, playing all the characters, even the animals and inanimate objects. I was in the zone and right at home.

I'm the same today. Still can't sing. Still crush charades.

Well-Oiled Improv Machine

My teammates know me. When it's time for someone to get physical, play an animal or act out a clue in an improv guessing game, I'm the go-to guy. When it's time for music, Elijah is the man. Others are good at foreign accents, creating characters, amazing wit and puns, riffing with the audience, or moving the scene forward and developing story.

We know each other, we are in tune with what the scene needs and we yield to one another's strengths. More than that, we work to set each other up for success. We purposefully direct the scene, in the moment, to include opportunities for someone to shine.

When my team yields to me on stage it's not because I'm the boss, it's because that's the best way to move forward in that moment. Thirty seconds later

I'll likely be supporting another actor's moment to shine. Leading in circles around a central purpose. In our case, an incredible improv performance.

When everyone agrees on the purpose and is willing to yield for the sake of progress, it's easy to get everyone going in the same direction. Leading in circles. Kind of like a roundabout.

Stoplights and Roundabouts

The area I live in has been in the process of changing a number of intersections to roundabouts. Stop and go is being replaced by flow. Instead of taking turns—stopping on red, going on green—cars enter simultaneously from all directions. The definition of a roundabout is "a type of circular intersection or junction in which road traffic flows almost continuously in one direction around a central island."[3] You simply yield to the vehicle already in the roundabout.

How would you describe your leadership style? Are you a stoplight or a roundabout?

Stoplight Leaders

Do you feel the need to have a say on every decision? Does it trouble you when people move on an idea or project without getting the green light from you? Do you feel like everything will go well as long as you're there to say, "Slow down, wait, now go."?

Then I would say you are a stoplight leader.

Stoplights can be great leaders. Your experience and direction keep things running smoothly. The thing is, stoplight leaders can create a lot of frustration for their team. Having to wait for a green light on every little decision can feel suffocating.

It's not ideal for leaders, either. When you are involved in the base level details of every decision you lose sight of the big picture. When you spend time acting as a stoplight for your team you lose opportunities to lead from your own areas of strength and effectiveness.

Stoplight leaders have a hard time caring for different personalities, too. There will be some on your team who are aggressive and love to race ahead into the unknown and figure things out as they go. There are others who like to plod carefully, weigh decisions and get it right the first time. Some like to follow the rules to a T while others push the boundaries.

The racers, plodders, rule followers and rule benders don't understand one another. The cautious drivers and aggressive drivers each think the other is an idiot. Nothing brings out the conflicting differences in your staff like the hierarchy of stoplight leadership. Ask everyone to work the same way at the same pace and you're asking for trouble.

A final potential issue with stoplight leadership is lack of ownership and accountability throughout your organization. When a stoplight stops working chaos ensues. Your team has become dependent on your direction. If you're not there, how are decisions made? Who tells the aggressive drivers to wait or the cautious drivers to move forward? Suddenly there's a three staff pile up in the middle of the project and progress stops.

Roundabout Leaders

Contrast the rules of a stoplight leader with the structure and flow of a roundabout leader. A roundabout leader isn't concerned with directing traffic. Your goal is to make sure that everyone is going the same direction around a central idea or purpose.

Roundabouts work when you respect the flow and know when to yield. A good roundabout leader creates an environment that relieves frustration for her team and is very freeing for herself. It's structure vs. rules.

The danger here is lack of direction or communication. Everyone in a roundabout has to know the deal. You have to know what a roundabout is and how it works. There is nothing more dangerous in a roundabout than a vehicle heading the wrong direction. Accidents happen when a car refuses to yield to others or stops to figure things out. It's the leader's job to clearly communicate your direction and purpose.

Know your team, get everyone on the same page, and let them go. Watch them enter and exit from all directions and yield to each other in the moment as they circle a central purpose. A properly working roundabout is a beautiful thing.

Skid Marks

A final thought on stoplights and roundabouts. Guess what else you'll find at just about every new roundabout? Skid marks. Tire trenches through the grassy island or streaks of rubber across the cobblestone center. Why? Because some people struggle to handle change. They approach the new roundabout like they always approach an intersection. They come to a dead stop, or they drive straight through the middle without slowing. When you begin to change from a stoplight leader to a roundabout leader, be prepared to encounter a few screeching tires and skid marks along the way. It may take a bit of time for your team to adjust to the new flow in your organization.

Chapter 2: Perspective

I scream, you scream…well, just me actually.

The first time I ever performed improv in front of a live audience I took my shirt off and screamed. I had blanked on stage, and that's how I faced fear and dealt with not knowing what to say or do next. Half-naked screaming.

It worked, kind of. I got an awkward laugh from the audience. I also completely blew up the scene, threw the other actors for a loop and killed any momentum we had built. Not my finest moment.

I am glad to report that my improv skills have come a long way in over twenty years. I would also like to be able to say that was the last time I took my shirt off on stage. But apparently I can't have my cake and eat it, too.

A big part of what I was missing in that first show was perspective. I didn't know how to deal with my own fear and ego. I wasn't respecting the process of improv and didn't trust the other actors to bail me out. My lack of trust and respect turned me into a bare-chested, bellowing idiot who wrecked everything.

Your perspective defines how you act. It defines how you see yourself and how you see and treat others. It also affects how others respond to you. Perspective is key.

Sometimes my perspective still gets me into trouble. I'm wired to see the funny in things. Always have been. That works well for me on stage as a comedian. Unfortunately, when I leave the stage I don't change much. I'm also a husband, father and friend. I go to the store, the bank and to church. I tend to find humor in things wherever I am and don't always do well at keeping my mouth shut.

Just a few days ago, my wonderful wife told me that the things I think are funny are not always funny to everyone else, and sometimes I should just keep my thoughts inside my head. My wife is usually right.

Maybe you can relate. Or maybe by the time you have finished this book you'll think my wife is absolutely right. To that I will say, "you should see the stuff I edited out. This is progress."

Height vs. Heart

Perspective got me through high school. I was what you call a "late bloomer". Not late as in we had to start dinner without you. Late as in dinner was over hours ago and we've already put away the leftovers. I was extremely small for my age.

People were always surprised when I told them how old I was. I was often mistaken for a girl on the phone, too. There is nothing more infuriating to a high school boy!

My freshman year was tough. I was teased, pushed and tossed into garbage cans. One time a senior, one of the worst thugs at school, approached me menacingly with a role of duct tape. When he reached me he paused and said to his idiot sidekick, "Nah, he's just too little," and moved on. I felt like an Israelite with lamb's blood around my locker frame. The bully of death had just passed me by.

Though I didn't enjoy being picked on by older kids, I was hurt the deepest by my close friend. Jeremy was an incredible artist. I mean truly incredible. One day for an art assignment on perspective he drew a picture titled "The World According to Andrew Bright".

There I was, in amazing life-like detail, as a tiny boy with a terrified expression in a room full of giant desks, chairs and other peoples' legs. The art teacher thought it was such a great drawing that he gave it an "A" and pinned it to the classroom bulletin board.

I was crushed. At home, my dad was ready to march into school and turn the teacher into abstract art. I told him I really wanted to handle it myself. I know it was tough on him. I also know he was proud of me.

That evening I re-read Psalm 139[4]—a passage I had gone to a lot for perspective. I read that God knew me and what was going on in my life. I read that I was created with care and intent and that God's works, including me, are wonderful. Then I read Psalm 46[5] where I took to heart that God is an ever-present help in trouble, even when it feels like my world is crashing around me. Perspective.

The next day I confronted the teacher, who took down the drawing. I also talked honestly to my friend. He said he was sorry, and we moved on.

The flawed perspective of others threatened to crush me. A right perspective rescued me. My body eventually grew. It just took a while for my height to catch up with my heart.

Who's The Bully Now?

The problem with perspective is that we only have one, our own. We don't truly have the ability to see through another's eyes. I could walk a mile in your shoes if you let me borrow them. But even ten miles would not give me access to the dreams, fears, emotions, history and experiences that make you, you.

When my wife, Karla, and I were newly married I was asked to be the speaker at a week of camp for kids from third to fifth grade. It sounded like a lot of fun, and I cherished the opportunity to speak truth into the lives of young kids.

One day at lunch I was sitting in the dining hall with my wife when I suddenly froze. Across the room I saw a large boy sporting a wicked grin as he leaned over a much smaller, younger boy who was trying to eat his lunch. I couldn't hear what the bully was saying but I could guess. Then I noticed the small boy wiping at tears.

A flood of memories and emotion suddenly crashed through my mind. Before I knew it I was out of my seat and moving across the dining hall. I put my hand on the bully's shoulder and asked the smaller boy, "Is this kid bothering you?" He nodded.

I turned to the bully, squeezed his shoulder and said through gritted teeth, "If you ever bother this boy again, if you ever talk to him again, if I see you even look at this boy again, I will tear your arms from their sockets and shove them down your throat. Are we clear?" Yep. I said that.

The bully immediately started crying. I nodded and winked at the smaller boy, who was staring at me like I was Superman, then I returned to my seat across the Dining Hall of Justice.

That's when I heard my wife ask, "What did you just do?" That's when reality hit me. I, a man in my twenties and the camp speaker no less, had just told a ten-year-old boy that I was going to rip his arms off and shove them down his throat. Oh boy. At that moment I didn't feel like Superman.

Minutes later I was standing in front of the camp director.

"I have to tell you something."

"Sure, what is it?"

"I just told one of your campers that I am going to tear his arms from their sockets and shove them down his throat."

[Chuckle] [Awkward pause] "...are you serious?"

"Yep." Then I gave the director a brief rundown of the encounter.

"Wow...okay...now what?"

Minutes after that I was out looking for the bully so I could apologize. But when I approached him he ran for some reason. So I chased him.

I wonder what the other kids and staff were thinking as they watched the camp speaker running across the lawn after a fifth grader shouting, "Hey! Stop! I'm not going to rip your arms off! I just want to talk to you!"

We did talk, and it was great. I gave a heartfelt apology. Then I told him my own story of being bullied frequently as a kid. He told me that he was bullied a lot too for being overweight.

Wow, I didn't see that coming. Turns out that was the reason he tried to strike fear into the hearts of other kids. Self-defense for his own hurting heart.

I shared Psalm 139 with him. We became great friends that week. I kept my job as camp speaker, he kept his arms and we both learned a lot about each other's perspective.

Why Your Perspective As A Leader Is So Crucial

A right perspective is strength and confidence. A right perspective doesn't shy away from conflict or cower at adversity because a right perspective is based in truth. There is nothing more powerful than truth.

As a leader you need truth for yourself and for others. There will be days (or weeks or months or maybe even years) that you will doubt yourself and your ability to lead. There may also be times that you think you have it all figured out when you really don't. A right perspective is key.

Your perspective greatly affects the success of your team, too. How do you perceive their person and ability? Do you value what each has to offer or are there some whom you dismiss before they've opened their mouth? How you perceive others affects how you respond to them.

Here's another important question. How does your team THINK you perceive them? Hopefully truth and perception align here, but sometimes they don't. I once worked with a leader who only communicated with his team when things were going wrong. Most every time the leader called his subordinates they were corrected, admonished or even chewed out.

In reality, the leader genuinely appreciated and valued his team, and he wanted them to succeed. In his view, he left them alone when they were doing well, and called to "help out" when they had messed up. As you can imagine the perspective of the majority of his team was very different. Based on their leader's communication they felt unappreciated, insecure in their jobs, and they dreaded any interaction with him.

Keep in mind that the way you respond to and communicate with your team will affect the way they perceive you, and the way they feel you perceive them. If truth and perception don't align here, you have some work to do as a leader.

Perspective-Killers

I started this chapter by recounting how my own skewed perception wrecked an improv scene.

Directing my flawed perception were fear and ego, two of the biggest momentum killers your team will ever face. Dig deep enough into any issue your team is working through, and you'll likely find either fear or ego at the root. Sometimes you'll find both.

Fear

Fear taunts us, stalls us, compares us to others who seem so much more equipped for success or are already more successful. Fear keeps us from voicing a great idea because we're worried it may be lame. Fear is like those stupid trick birthday candles that never really go out. Just when you think you've extinguished fear, it flickers back to life again.

Fear can also be like a horrible tattoo you got across your shoulder blades or lower back. You can't remember getting it and hate that it's there. You feel like everyone is snickering or judging when your back is turned. The only thing that could possibly be more painful and costly than doing nothing is doing what it takes to have it removed.

May I ask, "Why would you ever want to remove fear from your life?"

One time following a gig the guys and I were in the hotel and ended up watching an episode of *Bad Ink*.[6] In a nutshell, the show features people with horribly embarrassing or poorly done tattoos who go to some master artists for help. The tattoo artists miraculously turn the bad ink into creative, tactful masterpieces. They don't remove the bad tattoos. They build over and around them.

We need to handle fear the same way. If our goal is to remove fear from our lives, then every time it flickers to life again we've failed. Rather, we build around the fear, master it and turn it to our advantage.

Personally, I love fear. I'm a thrill seeker. The higher, faster and more dangerous something is, the more I am drawn to it.

Even if skydiving and bungee jumping isn't your thing, my guess is that everyone embraces fear to some degree. Just think of how many people enjoy suspenseful movies. Take a minute to consider why roller coasters are so popular. Have you ever seen a billboard advertising the safest, slowest rollercoaster in the country?

Come Experience The Tranquilizer! Gentle Slopes. Tedious Turns. Nothing Matches the Monotony of the Tranquilizer! Buy a Day Pass And Receive a Souvenir Pillow!

Nope. Not interested.

I had the privilege of watching my boys, ages five and seven, experience Disneyland's Space Mountain for the first time this year. They took some time deciding whether or not they wanted to ride it. As we got closer to the front of the line and began to hear the sound of the cars on the track and the screams of the riders, I could see them beginning to feel apprehensive. I had told them we could get out of line and skip the ride at any time, but they wanted to go on.

During the ride one of them screamed his head off, and the other was so terrified he was completely silent. The photo waiting at the end of the ride was absolutely priceless. Better yet, they couldn't wait to do it again. It had been terrifying and exhilarating. We rode it several more times.

Everest vs. Escalators

It's the hard things that are the most rewarding. If I told you I had reached the summit of Mount Everest I'll bet you would be impressed. That's a short list of climbers. If I posted a picture on Facebook of me standing at the top of an escalator with the caption, "Victory! I did it! Bucket list checked!" would you still be as impressed? Not likely.

Being fear-less, as in without fear, sounds pretty boring. I'm not talking about fear from genuine danger like the fear of being harmed by someone. I'm talking about the fear that flickers to life, or maybe even envelopes us, when we're facing hard decisions or taking a leap into new territory.

I'm scared right now. Honestly. I have been battling fear throughout the entire process of writing this book. Sometimes it's fleeting, other times it has felt debilitating. Who am I to write a book on leadership? I'm a comedian, not a leader. There are so many others who are so much more qualified. I should be writing a book on how to get a musical family to play charades.

Before writing, I started scrolling through a number of other writers' websites and e-books and fell headlong into what best selling author Jon Acuff calls "The Comparison Trap." Rather than be inspired by other people's work, I became consumed by how unqualified I am to write my own. What was supposed to be inspiring only got me perspiring.

So yes, I'm battling fear in this book. That's also what's driving me. As I climbed out of the comparison trap I took a cue from Seattle Seahawks quarterback, Russell Wilson, and thought, "Why not me?" [7] Wilson is small as quarterbacks go, and many teams overlooked him. He wasn't drafted by the Seahawks until late in the third round. He wasn't drafted to be a starter either. He fought for it in training camp and won the job. Two years later the Seahawks won the

Super Bowl with Wilson at the helm. Their team mantra that year was "Why not us?"

So why not me? I truly believe that I have something important, unique and of value to offer readers. More than failure, I fear complacency or giving up.

I was terrified when I quit a public relations job to become a full-time comedian. The only thing that scared me more was not trying. I was scared that someday I would be looking out the corner office window of a big PR firm wondering what it would have been like to be a professional comedian. What would it have been like to be on stage making people laugh? To be watching them holding their stomachs, rubbing their jaws and wiping their eyes. To see the smiles and hear the exhausted sighs that follow a huge laugh and let me know I've done my job.

Well, I'll tell you.

It's incredible.

I love it.

It was a terrifying decision and it was the right one. This fits me. I don't regret the decision one bit.

All the amazing writers you love were once simply men and women with great ideas who had the courage to put themselves out there. Jon Acuff fought though fear with each of the books he has written. He says in his latest book, New York Times Best Seller *Do Over,* "You're reading my fifth book and I experienced more fear about writing this one than any of the others."[8]

He's talking about the book Seth Godin called the "Best career book ever written."[9]

It's an incredible book. It's one of the main reasons I'm writing this one. Thank you, Jon, for not giving up. I don't just mean on *Do Over*. I mean on your fourth book, your third book, your second book and especially your first book.

Jon wrote his way through fear. I am writing my way through fear. What has you scared? More importantly, what are you going to do with it?

Rather than fearing fear, let's embrace the discomfort and intensity it can bring and use it to drive us. Rather than working to remove it from our lives, let's take a note from the artists of *Bad Ink*. Let's build around it and turn it into something awesome.

I'll tell you exactly how to do that in just a bit, but first we need to deal with your ego.

Leggo My Ego!

Actors and comedians with big egos are horrible at improv. I've worked with them. That's why I'll take a great team player over a stand-out star any day. There is no "I" in "improv."

Where fear says, "I can't," ego says, "I won't, or "You can't". When you are not willing to give value to another person's idea, when you refuse to yield to someone else's lead, you're in trouble.

The more you overlook or disregard others on your team, the more you cut away at the lifeline you will need when you hit bottom. Whether out of anger, mistrust, or maybe self-preservation, your team will withdraw from you.

Don't call ego confidence when it's not. I've heard that before. "I'm just really confident." I know a lot of genuine, humble, confident men and women. I also know ego when I see it. The difference is how you see and treat others. Perspective.

When you refuse to assign value to someone else's voice based on sex, age, race, religion, economic status, their position in the company, or simply whether or not you get along with them, that's ego. When you hear what people say but aren't really listening, that's ego. Yes, there is a difference between listening and waiting for someone else to finish talking so it's your turn again. When you create rules for your organization based on how you like to operate rather than on what is the best way for your team to move forward, that's ego, too.

Confidence operates within grace and truth. That means even when the truth calls for tough love, it is delivered with respect and value. Ego operates within fear and exclusion.

You: "Wait, did you just bring it back to fear? Weren't we talking about ego?"

Me: "Yes, to both."

Sometimes what looks like ego is actually fear. Like the pretty girl that everyone assumes is stuck-up when in reality she is painfully shy. Like me. Not the pretty girl part, but the fear masquerading as ego part.

Excellence is a big deal to me. It's a big deal to everyone in The Panic Squad Improv Comedy. Has been since day one. I think one of the reasons we have done well is our consistent desire to be excellent on and off the stage.

There are times, however, when my desire for excellence turns me into a control freak who runs over others. I've done it with my team and I've done it at home. Not something I'm proud of.

I get scared that excellence is going to suffer if everything isn't going according to plan (my plan). So I push forward on my terms and disregard the ideas of others. I can try to justify my actions by telling myself it's my right as the boss and that I have the most to lose when things go sideways. Both are true. I am the boss and do have the most to lose, but being technically accurate doesn't excuse poor actions.

In truth, I really have the most to lose when I don't take care of my team. Because the thing I'm driving on, no matter how noble the intent, is never as important as the relationship I may be destroying. Fear can breed ego. Ego wrecks everything.

That's what happened to me on stage during my very first live improv show. I was operating as a star performer, not a team player. When I blanked I figured since it was my problem it had to be my solution. I was focused on I and Me. That's not improv, nor is that leadership.

The Improv Perspective – A Better Way

I still blank on stage sometimes. Everyone does. I handle it differently though. Now, when I blank on stage I simply give my teammates a look they recognize that says, "I've got nothing."

Then whoever has an idea takes the lead, and I support them. Later on I may bail someone else out. Trust and respect are such an integral part of our team that no one cares who is leading or following. We know that as long as we are all a part of the process, it's going to be awesome.

I trust that each person on my team knows how to create a great improv scene. I trust that they care about excellence and, therefore, have my best interest in mind the same way I am working to support them.

When I'm on stage with The Panic Squad Improv Comedy, I can do anything—even blank in the middle of a scene—and it's going to be great. This is a wonderful place to be.

You can get there, too, by working to make trust and respect an integral part of your team. It will squash fear and ego. It will make you a leader your team wants to follow.

Does your team know it's okay to be scared when you're doing big things? Do you trust your staff enough to tell them that sometimes you're scared too? One of the great things about trust and respect is that when it is freely and unconditionally given, it is usually reciprocated.

Make Me An Offer

There is a very simple way trust and respect is formed in improv comedy—accepting offers. An offer is simply an idea to move the scene forward. Since there is no script, momentum depends on the team's ability to build on each other's ideas and move forward.

If you and I were on stage together I may say to you, "Let's barbecue steaks tonight." That's an offer. Now you have a choice. You can agree with me or shut me down.

Fear and ego tell you to shut me down. Maybe you have never barbecued anything in real life and are scared you will look stupid. Or maybe you're a dedicated vegan and you're worried that if you do a scene involving meat, you may throw up on stage. So you shut me down. That's fear.

Then again, maybe you've decided you want the scene to be about painting the house instead. That's a better idea in your mind. So you shut down my inferior idea. That's ego.

As soon as an idea is shut down, momentum stops. We're back to square one. You've also destroyed the trust between actors. You have essentially told me you don't value my ideas and refuse to support me. Ouch.

Your other option is to agree with me. You still know nothing about barbecuing and you're still worried that you may throw up the Quinoa you had for lunch. You also understand that the only way to move this scene forward is to accept my offer and build on it with your own idea.

More important than your fear of steak or your desire to paint the house is your commitment to the scene and to me, your teammate. You decide to respect the process and trust that I will be as supportive of you as you are of me.

"Let's barbecue steaks tonight."

"That sounds like fun. Have you ever had tofu steaks before?"

"No, but I'd love to try them. I'll start the barbecue."

"I'll grab a hedge trimmer."

"What's the hedge trimmer for?"

"To carve the tofu steaks."

"That sounds fun!"

"Grab your weed eater and we'll make some ground beet burgers, too."

...and we're on our way to a fantastic improv scene.

Yes And

This scene building principle is called "Yes And." YES I accept your idea AND I am willing to build on it with an idea of my own. It's one of the very first improv exercises I teach to rookie actors. I also include Yes And in a number of my corporate workshops.

Here's how it works. I break people into pairs and give everyone a simple offer to start with. Something like, "Let's go to the mall." Partner A starts with the original offer. Partner B must respond, "Yes, And..." and add an idea of their own. Then it's back to Partner A.

It looks like this:

A: Let's go to the mall.

B: Yes, And... I'll invite my grandfather.

A: Yes, And...we'll ask him to drive.

B: Yes And... we'll use the gas money we save to buy him new black socks.

A: Yes And... then we'll donate his old socks to science.

The story can go on for as long as you like. When you are playing Yes And you are doing improv. You are accepting your teammate's offers and building on them with your own ideas. That's improv.

Anyone can do it. It's a fact I've proven in every workshop I teach. The really fun part is, though everyone starts with the same original offer, from that point on no two stories are the same because no two teams are the same.

How Yes And Will Help You Lead

As a leader you need to regard each of your team members with a Yes And perspective. I'm not saying you have to agree with everything that comes out of their mouth. We're talking about perspective.

Yes And is a perspective of alignment. We are going to create something great together. I need you in order to do this just as you need me. I will be listening for what you have to offer, and I will trust you with my ideas.

Yes And is a perspective that assumes the best in people or makes no assumptions at all. It assigns inherent value to another's ideas. A leader who holds a Yes And perspective is eager to hear the ideas of his team and is grateful there are others on this journey with him.

How would you like to work with a leader who values your input, is aligned in purpose and who expects great things to come from working together? Sounds wonderful, doesn't it?

Yes But...

After we play Yes And in our workshops, we immediately play Yes But. It's the exact same exercise, save for one change. We replace the word "and" with "but." That's it.

The difference is incredible. Partners struggle to work together. Stories continually stall instead of flow. As we debrief the two exercises it becomes clear that just as Yes And is aligning in nature Yes But is dividing. I hear comments like, "It felt like we kept butting heads."

Well, that's exactly what's going on. Yes but is argumentative by nature and assumes the worst. We are essentially saying to one another "YES that's a fine idea BUT here is where it is flawed or here is a better idea." A leader who holds to a Yes But perspective will hear the ideas of his team but feels the need to correct, adjust or simply disregard the input.

A Beautiful Example

Here is a crystal clear example. Let's say that my incredible wife comes up to me and asks, "Do you think I am beautiful?" Let's look at my options.

"Do you think I am beautiful?"

"Yes, And..."

My options here are limitless. I could also tell her what a wonderful mother she is to our four kids. I could compliment her innate business sense or her ability to save our family money. I could tell her how much I appreciate her desire to grow in her faith and encourage me to do the same. All are true, by the way. My wife is incredible.

Or I could go with option two.

"Do you think I am beautiful?"

"Yes, but..."

I've already lost, haven't I? There is no recovery from this. I have completely erased the fact that I find her beautiful by following up with "but." I mean really, what am I going to say?

"Yes, but you used to be prettier."

"Yes, but you smell bad."

"Yes, but I hate your hair."

Technically, when asked whether or not I thought my wife was beautiful, I said "Yes." But are any of those statements a compliment? Are any of those statements affirming or loving?

Yet that's how many leaders see their team. "I value Bill's ideas, but...(insert statement on work history, personality, past issues etc.)" Say whatever you want then add "but," and it completely destroys any positive statement you were trying to make.

When you approach your team with a Yes But perspective, you devalue them. You may appear to be aligning, but you are working against them. You are in effect saying, "Yes, I am listening, but I probably won't agree with you or value your ideas."

Why is that? Why are there those on your team whom you meet with a Yes But attitude? Is it past mistakes, lack of experience, general mistrust, professional or personal envy, a grudge? Whatever the reason, you are destroying trust and respect, setting a horrible example for the rest of your team and ruining your chance to create something incredible together.

If you really want to lead your team well, you have to be willing to adjust your perspective. The right perspective can turn you into an authentic, effective leader whom your team eagerly follows. A false or negative perspective will erode your ability to lead well.

Work to discover the truth. There is nothing more powerful than truth. What is the truth about who you are? What is the truth about your team, both as individuals and as a group? Find truth and use the Yes And perspective to cultivate trust and respect. You'll be amazed with the way your team and you are transformed.

Chapter 3: Direction and Structure

It was a size eleven Birkenstock sandal, and I'll never forget it.

I am intimately familiar with this sandal.

During a show for the student body at Trinity Western University in British Columbia, Canada, this sandal came flying out of the darkness beyond the stage lights and hit me in the face. I went down. I had a mark on my face for four days.

Every improv scene starts with an "ask for". The actors ask the audience for an idea to start the scene. Some examples are:

What's a unique first job?

Where is a horrible place to play hide and seek?

What's a good reason to celebrate?

What's something you'd find in your grandmother's attic?

By the way, if your answer to that last question was "grandfather", you're not as creative as you think. We get that ALL the time.

At the TWU show, rather than deliver the "ask for" as a question, I simply said, "Give me something you'd find in your closet." Most of the students started shouting out ideas. One person, a young man named Richard, took my statement literally.

Richard decided to actually give me something from his closet and hurled his size 11 Birkenstock from the top of the bleachers where he was sitting. Seconds later the crowd gave a collective "OOOH!" and I was on the floor.

I know his name is Richard because a year or two later I received an email that began, "You don't know me, but I'm the guy who hit you in the face with my shoe." He apologized and explained that he didn't try to hit me, he was just trying to be funny. Yep, I can relate. All was forgiven. Richard got to make his mark, on my face, and now he's in my book, too. Nice work Richard.

Direction and Structure

Direction is important. If your team doesn't know exactly what you're asking of them, you might not end up with the result you were expecting. You may even get hit in the face with a shoe.

You don't have the right to be upset at your team for going off course if you haven't told them what it means to win and how to get there.

In chapter one we talked briefly about getting everyone going the same direction. Let's revisit and expand on the importance of that. Direction is essential. A roundabout only works when we're all flowing the same way around it. As a leader, it's important for you to clearly communicate the direction you are taking your team. Direction tells you where you've come from, where you are, and where you're going.

Structure is the framework and process that gets you there. Using the roundabout analogy, structure is the lanes, arrows, signs and rules that allow your team to move freely and efficiently. Without structure flow stalls and chaos ensues.

Direction

For The Panic Squad Improv Comedy, we work to create an amazing improv show that entertains the audience and delights the client. That looks different onstage than it does offstage. Both are all about excellence.

We also teach workshops on leadership, teamwork and stage communication. Each is different but our purpose and direction are the same. Our goal is to care for the client and deliver excellence. Be it a performance, client/fan relationship or a workshop, my team has to know what excellence looks like and how we get there.

Well-oiled Pancake-making Machine

I use a very fun, clear exercise to teach this principle in my workshops. It's called "Machines". I ask for 5 volunteers to join me in the front of the room. I line them up side-by-side, facing the rest of the group, and tell them they are each a part of a machine that makes something great. I don't define the "thing" for them. Each person has to decide what the machine will be making and keep it to themselves.

I ask the person on one end to begin making a sound effect and repetitive motion that relates to what they are making. There is no talking allowed. The next person then has to come up with their own sound effect and motion, and on down the line. It looks like an assembly line. The person on the far left is the beginning of production and the person on the far right is the end result.

It's pure chaos. Nothing makes sense. It's hilarious for the staff who are watching as the "machine" whizzes, whirs, clangs and booms. I let this go on for about a minute then stop the action so we can debrief.

First I ask those watching what they think the machine was making. People offer some fun guesses, but no one has a clue. Then I ask the volunteers themselves what they were making and what their specific job was.

Most often, everyone has a different idea. Sometimes people playfully argue, incredulous that their teammate could not understand what they were doing.

"How could you not know I was recycling tin cans?!"

"How could YOU not know I was filling a box with Styrofoam peanuts?!

Now comes the interesting piece. I tell the volunteers that we are going to create another machine but with one change. This time I am going to tell them what the machine makes. It is a machine that makes pancakes.

Once again their job is to make a specific sound effect and action. The person on the far left begins production. The person on the far right is the end result. GO!

The difference is absolutely incredible. Now that we all know where we're headed, each person easily finds their role. Eggs are cracked, batter is mixed, ladles spoon batter onto the griddle, pancakes are flipped and 90% of the time, the last person adds syrup and eats one.

There is still no talking allowed. Yet it's a beautifully operating machine. When I stop the machine, I first ask the rest of the staff what they think each person was doing. They all know. John was cracking eggs, Sara was stirring the batter, etc.

Amazing, isn't it? When you introduce direction, each person's task becomes clear to themselves, clear to the rest of their team and even clear to those who are watching. It's a well-oiled machine.

As a leader, take time to ensure your team has clear direction. Without direction, confusion and chaos reigns. With clear direction, you will be amazed at how quickly and easily your team will find their roles. Everyone on your team should be able to say with confidence, "We make pancakes." Or whatever it is that you really do.

Finding Your Direction

One way to get everyone on the same page and headed the same way is to ensure a crystal clear understanding in three areas:

History – Where have we come from?

Mission – What are we about and how do we operate?

Vision – Who do we want to be and where do we want to go?

Humble Beginnings

The Panic Squad's history is humble but is also important for who we are today. The Panic Squad officially started in April of 1996. A few friends from college and I were just trying to do more of what we loved. Improv Comedy.

We performed anywhere we could. If a youth group needed entertainment, we were there.

Occasionally we did a sports banquet or small corporate function. We usually made about $25 each.

When we started out we set two standards right off the bat.

Number one, we would only perform clean comedy. In our view, God gave us the ability to be really funny. It made sense to honor Him with those gifts. We also think that clean comedy is more difficult and more rewarding than base humor.

Second, we wanted to be excellent in everything we did. That means we had to care about every aspect of the show, both on and off the stage, and give it our best. Clean comedy that is truly excellent.

Our first self-promoted, ticketed show was a joint venture with a Christian coffee house/theatre in New Westminster, British Columbia. Six people showed up. Two were an actor's parents. Two were another actor's roommates. Two were actually strangers who chose to come to our show without feeling obligated.

Our agreement was to split the door sales with the coffee house. Tickets were only $2 each, so our half of the take was $6. We split that equally between the 5 actors that performed that evening. That's $1.20 each. Humble beginnings for sure.

Something important happened that evening though. We were feeling discouraged backstage. We didn't necessarily want to go out and perform a ninety-minute show for six people. Then we reminded each other about the decisions we had made regarding what The Panic Squad Improv Comedy is about. We owed these six people an excellent show, and we decided to give it to them.

We took the stage with energy and performed our hearts out for those few people. That's what excellence does. We were not going to let the size of the audience dictate the quality of our performance. Four months later we were breaking fire codes with over five hundred people coming to our shows.

Two actors moved on and three of us continued to perform clean and hilarious improv comedy shows. We worked hard. In 2001 we quit our jobs and became full-time comedians.

Since that first public show we have performed all across Canada and in forty states. We've performed for diverse audiences ranging from local churches and businesses to large national conferences and top Fortune 500 Corporations.

Audiences have ranged from the original six to over 35,000. More importantly, over the 20 years The Panic Squad has been performing, we have entertained literally hundreds of thousands of people across North America with hilarious, clean comedy.

Excellence has paid off. I'm proud to say we have an exceptional track record. We've also failed miserably over the years and have learned from our mistakes. That is a part of our history, too.

Our history and commitment to excellence is something every performer on The Panic Squad understands. When I face tough hurdles now, I'll often think back to that first show for six people. What if we had cancelled the performance and went home? What if we had given up?

What is your story? What about your journey will reveal something important about who you are as a person and an organization? Your team needs to hear the story often.

Mission and Vision

Let's start with vision. One thing I love about the unscripted nature of improv is that anything is possible. I love that fact that I never know what is going to happen on stage, but I know it's going to be great. I love laughing on stage, in the middle of the show. It means I've been so surprised by something another actor has said that I burst out laughing. I expect every show to be excellent, but sometimes it is so surprisingly great that we all just have to stop and laugh. The audience loves it, too. Those are great moments.

What would create that kind of moment for you? Dream with me a little bit. In your organization, what would be such an amazing accomplishment or milestone that the only thing you can do is shake your head and laugh? Last year's data didn't forecast it, your team can hardly believe it, but it happened. And you're laughing. It's humbling and awesome, and the thought of it just a makes you giggle.

Well, why not? What's stopping you and your team from accomplishing great things? Could it be that these wonderful goals and ideas only live inside your head? It is important to communicate your big ideas to your team and work those ideas into your vision as a company.

Next is your mission? Who are you as a company and what are you trying to do? More importantly, why are you doing it? If you want to do truly great things as a leader, you have to have a team who is on the same page and headed the same direction. To do that, everyone has to know who you are as an organization and how you operate.

It's worth your time, if you haven't already, to sit down and define your mission for yourself and for your team. Then make sure everyone knows what it is. Post it in common areas, talk about it often, and highlight what it looks like in your specific organization to follow the mission. Give some practical examples of how to work in a way that is aligned with your mission. Point out some employees who are getting it right. Make sure your team understands where you're headed and why, and can define what winning is. When your team members have a solid grasp of your history, mission and vision, it's easier to get everyone going in the same direction.

Your Unique Is Better Than Somebody Else's Awesome

There are times in an improv show where we really knock it out of the park. The scene is smooth, witty, and hilarious. It would make sense to try to reproduce that scene the next time we get a similar suggestion from the audience. We actually get similar suggestions all the time. When we ask an audience to shout out creative household items they often shout out the same creative suggestions the last audience gave us. It's funny how similar people are across the country.

We have tried to re-create awesome scenes in the past. The audience in St. Louis would never know we're doing the same scene in Seattle. Unfortunately, every time we tried to reproduce a great scene it failed miserably. For one, we never quite got it right. It's like following your grandma's recipe and missing a pinch of this or adding a bit too much of that. The bigger problem was method and creativity. When you are remembering, you are not creating. They are different processes.

Improv is all about creating something together. When you are being creative with a trusted team wonderful things can happen. When you are trying to reproduce something that was awesome before or was awesome for someone else, you're not creating anymore. You're imitating. Imitating excellence can be more difficult for your team than creating excellence with your team.

Pastor and leadership expert Carey Nieuwhof discusses this idea in his book, *Impact—7 Powerful Conversations That Will Help Your Church Grow*.

"Imitation has killed innovation. Because we live in a digital age when church leaders easily keep their fingers on the pulse of what other church leaders are doing, we also find ourselves living in the age of imitation."[10]

Nieuwhof says that while he sees the value in learning from others and borrowing great practices, church leaders rarely imitate all the best practices. He goes on to say, "Too many times we're looking for silver bullets, tricks, or gimmicks that will move our church into a growth phase...What's needed now more than ever is church leaders willing to pioneer, to go deep into a culture that keeps changing to reach people who are increasingly resistant. What's needed most as we look at what's ahead is innovation."[11]

The same can be true for your organization. Have you replaced innovation with imitation? Have you discovered that your version of grandma's recipe just isn't the same as she makes it? Maybe the best thing your team has going is not the thing that other's are doing well, it's the thing that is unique to you. Create with your team. Learn from others, but find your own awesome.

In communicating your mission and vision to your team, be real. Be unique. Be you.

Once you have clearly communicated history, mission and vision to your team, you have entered the roundabout and are beginning to see some flow. Everyone is headed the same way. Now we need to add some structure so we can spend our time on things that matter, build some momentum and keep from crashing into to one another in the process.

Spontaneous Structure

We have a number of strong structural practices and systems in improv comedy.

Wait, what?

Isn't improv a free flowing organic genre of acting and comedy that is unscripted and spontaneous by nature?

Yes, that's true.

No two improv scenes are ever the same. We are creating in the moment for the first time every time. Improv is the essence of creativity and spontaneity.

Improv also has an important structure that makes a scene work or self-destruct. Follow the formula and you win. Forget where you are and you lose. The basic structure for a good improv scene is as follows:

1. **Environment** - Where are you and what are you doing?

2. **Characters** – Who is in the scene and what is their relationship?

3. **Conflict** – Get into trouble. Make something happen.

4. **Raise the stakes** – Make it worse, bigger or more important.

5. **Conclusion** – Wrap it up.

Each improv scene must have these components to be successful, and we work to create them in the order listed. We set up the environment—be it a kitchen, a forest or a Pilates studio. We add interesting characters who will at some point discover a conflict. We make the issue bigger to bring the audience to the edge of their seats. Then we find a conclusion and end the scene.

This all happens in three to five minutes. Then we get another "ask for" from the audience and do it all again. A completely different, yet equally complex and hilarious, scene using the same basic structure. Within that framework is plenty of room for creativity. The structure is also a roadmap for when we get lost in the scene. Where are we? What's next? Okay go.

Because a framework is in place and we all know what it is, we are free to be creative with the things that matter. Instead of wasting our energy trying to remember how to do improv, we simply get to do improv and create incredible comedy within a proven structure.

Scripted Improv

The Panic Squad takes the whole systems and structure thing a step or two further. We script our show intro, game intros and other transitions. It's the same every time. We want the parts of our show where we are explaining or introducing something to be clear and concise.

We don't want to waste time trying to remember how to introduce a specific improv game. An improv show takes an immense amount of mental energy. We want to use that energy for the fun stuff, creating. We also want to make sure we're clear. We need the audience to be tracking with us.

Do you have a standard email response or template for a request you get over and over again? All you have to do is personalize it a bit, and you're done. You've answered the request with excellence and efficiency, and you're free to do other work. Same idea.

In The Panic Squad we even have a system for audience banter, the most fluid and organic part of our show. Bantering with the audience is a wonderful tool to create relationship, and really personalize the performance. We comment on something that just happened in the previous scene. We chat with an audience member. We poke fun at one another. It's a lot of fun and very entertaining.

Years ago we discovered that we were all so eager to join in the banter that we ended up talking over each other or interrupting someone else's transition. That wrecked the flow of the show and made us look bad. So we came up with a simple system that allows us to freely banter without looking unprofessional. I won't divulge what the system is; that's not important. The point is we created it to improve the part that matters, the ability to successfully create relationship with the audience while maintaining the quality and momentum of our show.

Other artists are the same. A painter may have a certain way he lays out his brushes and arranges his paint so he is free to create a masterpiece. A musician may have a system to the way she writes lyrics, develops a melody, or simply gets herself into the zone so she can create music that moves people.

What systems or structures do you need to put into place to free your team to be creative and do important work? What does great work look like for your team? Can you define it and break it down into three to five parts that act as a roadmap or picture of excellent work? If you can do this, then you can create a structure for great work in your church or business. Now you have something to refer to and check yourself against when you're in unknown territory. Now you have lanes and a few rules to keep everyone moving without fishtailing or crashing.

Creativity does not mean chaos. Being on the leading edge does not condone inefficiency. Create a structure that speeds success.

If I were Confucius I may say something like, "Even man who bounces off walls must still have walls to bounce from." I'm not Confucius, though. I have more in common with the man bouncing off the walls.

Structure allows for creativity. Framework enables flow. Give your team clear direction and help create a structure that will enable success in the moment.

The Water Nazi

Be careful not to mistake rules for structure. I have nothing against rules. Rules are important when tied to a purpose. But rules for rules' sake can be exhausting and debilitating. Find a person who lacks initiative and reeks of indifference, and I'll bet you'll find a web of rules suffocating the service out of them.

One of the perks of traveling often and having a lot of air miles is the occasional free upgrade to first class. A number of years ago I was sitting in first class aboard one of the major airlines. It was nice. I had a wide, cushy seat and lots of legroom. There was a small bottle of water waiting for me in the center armrest.

As I was in my recliner watching the peasants and commoners board, I saw an older gentleman and his wife step onto the plane. The man did not look well. He was red-faced and sweating. As he boarded he asked the flight attendant, "May I have some water, please?"

She apologized and said that the service cart would be by once the plane took off and reached cruising altitude. She said she would be happy to get him some water then. If you fly often, you know that's about 20 minutes after the plane takes off.

The man asked again, explaining that he really wasn't feeling well and added, "Can't I just have one of those little bottles, there?" The flight attendant was standing in front of several cases of mini bottles of water stacked in the front galley. Without wavering, the flight attendant gave the exact answer she had given previously.

Now the man's wife chimed in from behind him. "Please!" she said, "He needs to take his heart medication!" Ok, that should do it. There is a sick looking man boarding your plane who needs to take his heart medication. You have cases of water behind you. I know what I would do.

Unfortunately, the flight attendant did just the opposite. Again, she recited the cart service at cruising altitude script. This time she added, "Please take your seats so we can continue boarding. The faster we get this plane off the ground the sooner I can bring you some water."

The sick man in need of heart medication and his appalled wife began to move down the isle. As they passed my seat I silently held out my unopened bottle of water. The man took it and they both thanked me. A minute later, when there was a break in boarding traffic, I got the flight attendant's attention and asked, "May I please have another bottle of water?"

"Certainly!" she said with a smile. She reached behind her, took a bottle and walked it to my seat. Then she asked if I needed anything else.

Consider how shocked you are reading this. Imagine watching it unfold. I really don't think the flight attendant was cold or mean spirited, though her actions made her appear that way. I'm sure that the airline's rules dictated that passengers in coach are served during cart service. First class passengers can be served at any time.

I don't think that is an unrealistic rule. It's common among airlines, actually, and it makes sense. Flight attendants can't be running water, soda and coffee to hundreds of passengers while the plane is boarding. It would be chaos.

What makes no sense is the lack of flexibility within the rule. What is truly frustrating is the lack of decision-making power given to the employees on the plane. My guess is the flight attendant would have gladly given the man some water if she did not fear being reprimanded or penalized by the airline.

"I sincerely hope you don't die before I get you some water, sir, but I'm afraid I'll lose my job if I serve you. Last week another flight attendant was fired for doing CPR on a baby while the pilot was trying to point out an interesting landmark."

I am also fairly confident that the other passengers in line who witnessed the conversation would not feel slighted by not getting water for themselves.

"Hey! How come Mr. Heart Issue over there gets water but I don't!"

Sadly, I've witnessed jerks like that, too. But there are enough good, understanding people in the world to warrant an airline giving water to a heart patient and not everyone else on the plane. I would also venture that most flight attendants can handle determining when to make those calls.

Unfortunately, the airline must have decided this is not the case. How would that make you feel as an employee? "We don't feel you are intelligent enough to know when to give water away, so here is a rule we've come up with to keep you from messing up."

How about you? Do you impose ridiculous rules on your team? Maybe you are not a Water Nazi, but are there rules or systems you have in place that are impeding your team from being great?

I'm all for rules with purpose. I just wrote a section on the structure and systems of improv. Actors who follow the rules have an easier time doing well on stage. That's because there is a purpose tied to each rule that moves the actor toward the end goal, a great improv scene. Rules with purpose align with your mission and create structure. A leader who creates rules for rules sake only hurts progress. That's why responsible government is an oxymoron. Rather, coach your team into understanding what matters most in your organization. A flight attendant, who knows her company values people above all else, feels free to help a man take his heart medication. She also understands that passengers are not served best by handing everyone a drink before takeoff.

The Hat That Roared

Before becoming a full-time comedian I worked for a marketing and public relations agency. My last year at the firm we worked on an intense project. An underground pipeline leak resulted in an explosion that killed three people. A very public legal battle ensued to see who was responsible. Was it the pipeline company, or a construction company who had done excavation work in the area and may have damaged the pipeline?

The firm I worked for represented the pipeline. We often had meetings that included a number of public relation officials from different firms, company leaders for the pipeline and other big wigs. One day while searching for something in our firm's storage area, I found an old box of hats bearing the construction company's logo.

Apparently they had ordered some promotional products through the marketing arm of our company several years prior. They were not a current client.

I had a good relationship with a number of the PR officials from our company and other companies involved, including the pipeline officials. They all appreciated that I was able to keep things light in the middle of such intense work. When I found the hats, I thought of a funny idea.

(A quick aside. I could write an entire book on things I have done that I thought were funny, that no one else did. Today I'll just mention this one.)

The next time we all came together for a meeting, I made sure I was the last to enter the boardroom. You guessed it. I was wearing the hat I found. The hat bearing the logo of the construction company that our current client was in an intense legal battle with.

It wasn't as funny as I thought it would be.

The air left the room. There were stares, a couple of nervous chuckles, and my boss's face was turning purple with anger. I quickly got rid of the hat. No one said anything else about it during the meeting.

Later that afternoon my boss called me into his office. We had a "discussion". He did most of the talking. I listened.

It turns out that following the meeting a flurry of phone calls were made as leaders who were at the meeting called their leaders, who called their lawyers, who called my boss. He told me that my little joke had cost the company roughly $5,000 in time and fees that were spent putting out the fire I started.

Thankfully we kept the client and, miraculously, I kept my job. My boss was a patient and gracious leader. I had made a horrible gaff that embarrassed him and cost the company money. So why didn't he make a new rule, "No more hats in the boardroom!" Would that not address the problem directly? Better yet, how about a "No more Andrew Bright in the boardroom" rule? That may have been more appropriate.

Instead, he chose to focus more on conduct than the situation. He talked to me about client relationships and how important it is to care for and protect them. We discussed the consequences our decisions bring about. He relayed the importance of being sensitive to other people and perspectives, especially when the issues are as intense as the ones we were dealing with.

He also told me I was an idiot and to never pull anything like that again. I can promise you I wasn't planning on it. Not because there was a new "no hats" rule in place. It was because I had gained a new understanding of client relationships, corporate etiquette, consequences and just plain common sense that I was lacking in my twenties.

When things go terribly wrong, some leaders are quick to make a new rule to fix it. Maybe what's needed more is better understanding of the issue and guidance in behavior. Train, don't regulate.

Let's Get Personal

Do you have personal rules that allow you to lead with excellence? I'm no longer talking about a system to do great work. I'm talking about a system to protect your heart and mind, which, by the way, are key in helping you do great work.

I do. So does my team. We give each other a HIP check from time to time. A hip check is a hockey term, and some of the guys on The Panic Squad love hockey. Our own HIP check has nothing to do with hockey. We just thought it was a cool name.

The Panic Squad HIP check stands for Humility, Integrity and Purity. Three things that are important to us as Christian men and entertainers. It's easy to fail in each area. So we give each other a HIP check. Sometimes we're just doing a general check-in with each other.

Other times we'll say, "Hey, I need to give you a HIP check on that" following a specific conversation or event. It keeps us accountable and headed in the right direction. It's the beauty of community.

I have some personal rules, too, that the other guys don't necessarily follow. I set my boundaries back farther than most others because I know I'm a people pleaser. I can see myself getting into an awkward situation because I don't want to offend anyone. So I take the situation-by-situation decision-making out of the equation and simply make a non-negotiable rule. This also protects me from making a poor decision when I'm tired, hurt or angry.

One such boundary is that I am never alone with a woman. Not in a car, not at a table in a restaurant, not for a meeting, not ever. It's one of those non-negotiable rules that most people don't subscribe to and that's fine. I don't expect it of anyone else nor do I look down my nose at anyone who feels differently. This rule just simplifies things for me, which I like. It also honors my wife, whom I love.

Sometimes it's awkward. One time I was performing at a large conference and was having lunch with Eric Samuel Timm,[12] a phenomenal artist and speaker, as well as a couple of employees from World Vision. Following lunch I needed to head back to the conference center. Eric wanted to stop by his hotel, and the World Vision guy was his ride. The other World Vision staffer, a young lady, also needed to get back to the conference. "No problem," she said. "I'll just catch a ride back with Andrew."

I had to explain that it was nothing personal, but I don't ever drive alone with women. I could tell it was weird for her, maybe even a bit offensive, and I apologized several times. She decided to ride with the other guys even though it would take extra time. I felt horrible. The people pleaser in me wanted to say, "Okay, just this once should be fine." I honestly wasn't worried about either myself or the young lady. It was simply a non-negotiable, personal rule I had set.

Just as I was feeling like a bit of a dirt-bag and questioning my rule, Eric pulled me aside, and I'll never forget what he said. "Andrew, you should never apologize for honoring your marriage and showing love and respect to your wife."

You know, he's right. There are worse things for which I could have to apologize. My pastor gave me a bit of wisdom that I recall often. He said, "Use your sane moments to protect you from your insane moments."

How about you? What are some areas in your life that you may need to protect yourself from? You are a leader. People are watching.

I also believe that the man or woman you are on the inside directly affects how you lead. Protect your head and heart. Use your sane moments to create rules and habits that protect you from when you are tired, hurt, angry or simply looking for trouble.

Chapter 4: Create A Culture of Celebration

My family loves game shows. Our favorite game show is The Price Is Right.[13] The excitement is over the top. The audience is constantly cheering. It's contagious, and that's just through the TV screen. Can you imagine being there?

My wife can. She was on the Price is Right[14] last year along with her sister and a couple of our nieces. They had a wonderful time. My wife tells me you can't imagine the energy in the room. Everyone is constantly cheering and clapping, shouting and dancing. It's non-stop celebration.

You're rooting for your friends, too. Not just the people you came with, but just about everyone else there. You've been in line with these people for hours. Moved with them from room to room. You share a common bond—you love the show. And you share a common dream—to hear your name called.

By the time they start taping the show you have a whole new group of friends to cheer on. I think that's part of the reason there is so much energy in the room on The Price Is Right.

Celebrate The Ones You Love

I was invested in watching the show, too, when it finally aired months later. I had asked the ladies to please not tell me anything so I could experience it for the first time on TV. I love surprises. I couldn't wait to see what had happened. Most of all, I was excited to see my family on the show. I knew these people. I loved these people. I wanted to see them win.

We cheered when we saw my wife and the others clearly in the second row of the audience. There they were, on The Price Is Right. It was so cool.

Then my niece's name was called.

Then she gave the closest bid and got up on stage.

Then she won a car.

Then she landed on $1.00 in the Showcase Showdown.

Then she went on to the Showcase.

I was freaking out, jumping and cheering wildly as I watched the episode on TV. It was so much fun. I love to celebrate.

Winner, Winner Prime Rib Dinner!

I have a unique privilege being a professional comedian. I get to celebrate a lot. When a church or business wants to throw a big party they often bring in great entertainment. I get to go to a lot of wonderful celebrations.

December is basically a month-long string of parties as different groups host a banquet or corporate Christmas party. You know those incredible company dinners you have once a year with the prime rib and an entire buffet of delicious catered cuisine? I attended 14 of those dinners last December. I usually gain about 5 pounds throughout what The Panic Squad fondly calls "Buffet Season."

Besides the food and festive atmosphere, it's just plain fun to be around people at parties. Almost everyone is in a great mood. Whether it is a holiday, an annual meeting, a trip to celebrate a great year, a church creating a gala to thank their volunteers or a firm showing appreciation to their clients, it's all about rewarding people, honoring people, and saying thank you. It's so much fun to be a part of events designed to thank and honor others.

Celebrating is good for your team, too. Celebrating brings people together. Like laughter, celebration is something that is always better when shared. Celebrating recognizes good work, good people, and pushes your team to accomplish more.

Rock, Paper, Celebrate!

One of my favorite exercises I use to demonstrate the benefits of celebration is Rock Paper Scissors Entourage, or RPS Entourage for short. It's fast-paced, loud and so much fun.

I break the entire group into pairs. When I say "GO!" everyone does one round of Rock Paper Scissors. Whoever wins the battle puts their hand up and shouts, "Winner!" Whoever loses the battle becomes part of their former opponents entourage and cheers them on loudly in future battles.

The game moves quickly. Winners find each other and battle again. Losers AND their entire entourage are now cheering for the player that just beat them. The game culminates when there are only two opponents left, each with half of the room cheering them on wildly.

You would not believe how loud and crazy it gets, raising to a crescendo in the final battle. It's amazing. When we debrief I ask why everyone cheered so loudly for a simple game of Rock Paper Scissors. I get answers like:

"You're part of something bigger than yourself."

"You get caught up in the excitement."

"It was just really fun to be cheering with other people for your team."

"Even when you lose, you turn around and are suddenly on a team that you really want to win."

"More is at stake with every battle. The pressure is intense, but it feels so cool to have everyone cheering for you."

"When I won (the final battle) I felt like I had won the lottery. It felt amazing."

Consider that last statement, offered by the gentleman that won the entire game in the last workshop I taught. He and another player were at the front of the room surrounded by loud cheering sections. It was intense. The players were cracking their necks and shaking out their arms in preparation for the final battle. When he won his team erupted in jubilation and high-fives. He bellowed a victory cry with his arms raised. It was hilarious.

All over a little game of Rock Paper Scissors. Do you think he acts like this every time he plays Rock Paper Scissors? I asked him. He chuckled and said, "No".

Then what was the difference? Why did winning RPS Entourage feel like winning the lottery for this young man? The difference, we discovered, was in the entourage. It was in the momentum and intensity built by all the people cheering him on. The celebration itself created a new level of focus, intensity and fun.

RPS Entourage teaches us that when we work as a team to celebrate our wins and cheer on our teammates, we bring a higher level of motivation and encouragement to the table for everyone. It's human nature to push a little harder when we know someone is rooting for us and counting on us.

I learned this important lesson for myself just last month.

Aphids Up My Nose

I've always been creative, funny and relational. I'm good with people and I think I come up with a lot of good ideas. I really struggle with implementation, though. If I'm honest with myself, I have a hard time digging in and really hustling to get something done.

I'm not saying I'm lazy. I have accomplished some great things and am proud of who I am and what I've been able to do. I am also plagued by areas of regret where I left a great idea on the table, didn't jump on an opportunity or never got around to XYZ.

No one wants to be a workaholic and it's important to take time to smell the roses. If you don't, a lot of life passes you by while your nose is to the grindstone. That said, if you discover aphids living up your nose it's time to leave the rose garden and get something done.

A shift happened for me when I was listening to the Carey Nieuwhof Leadership Podcast[15] one afternoon. His guest, best selling author Jon Acuff, was discussing what hustle is and isn't and mentioned his 30 Days of Hustle Challenge[16]. It's an online training that teaches you how to set goals and get things done. It's full of helpful questions and motivating discussions and delivers some simple practical tools, as well. I know because I decided to take the course.

One thing I did not expect was the value and power of the private Facebook group for those enrolled in the course. Each day, including myself, members would post goals and updates. It was a very positive and encouraging group. We were all in the same boat, trying to learn something new, improve ourselves and get something done.

I felt for myself what I teach about celebration in my workshops. I pushed harder, did extra work, and avoided the rose bushes for a season because I knew people were rooting for me. It was incredibly motivating and encouraging. My goal was to finally create the blog[17] I had come up with over three years prior (aphids up my nose syndrome). I launched the blog on day 29 of the challenge.

Don't underestimate the power of rooting for your team. Not just in your head and heart but in real words and action. Get them rooting for one another. It will push them to greater things.

It builds, too. As your team grows closer through celebrating each other, they become more invested in seeing their team win. Think of me screaming my head off watching my niece win a car. I would be truly excited for you if you won a car, but I probably wouldn't jump and scream like a baboon on fire. I did for my family.

Introduce a culture of celebration into your work family.

Stop Cele-waiting and Start Celebrating!

So why aren't teams celebrating more? Why wait for the company Christmas party, the annual meeting or the volunteer gala? Maybe some leaders are hesitant to celebrate more often because there is still work to do. They don't want their team to lose focus.

There is time to work and there is time to celebrate. They are separate. Only after the crops are in do we celebrate the harvest.

I understand this sentiment, but I would argue that your team will actually gain focus and productivity when you learn to celebrate WITHIN the work, too.

What A Family Road Trip Taught Me About Celebration

I have four young children. Each summer we drive from our home in Northwest Washington to visit relatives in California. The drive is hours upon hours in the minivan and has the potential to be a nightmare of constant whining, fighting, crying and emergency potty breaks.

It's not. It's a great trip because my wife is brilliant. My wife turns our trip into a journey of celebration. One year she went to the local Dollar Store and bought a number of small toys and games. She also bought some inexpensive snacks. Every hour on the hour the kids would all celebrate. It was prize time. My wife would hand out either a little snack or a new little toy. The kids loved it. Sure, we answered the "What time is it?" question roughly a million times, but the drive was great. Our destination was our relatives' home, but the entire journey was seasoned with fun and anticipation.

Full disclosure: before you give us the perfect parent award, you should know that we have also had plenty of whining, fighting, crying and middle-of-nowhere emergency stops so someone could pee out the side door. But we're learning.

5 Real Benefits of Celebration

Become a leader who incorporates celebration INTO the work. Make it as much a part of the work as the goals, meetings, and daily tasks. Celebrate often within your project, as if it is woven into the fabric of who you are and what you do. Here are five wonderful benefits that will come from incorporating celebration into your daily work.

1. Your team will have more fun.

My friend Brent, who is an MD now, worked for a summer as a greens keeper for a golf course. Brent tells me one of the reasons he enjoyed the job was the attitude of the players. Why? They weren't at work. They were playing golf. This made them happy and fun to be around.

We like being around fun people. We like seeing a father who really loves his kids or a couple who is in love with each other. On the other hand it is difficult to be around people who don't like each other. Have you ever been invited to dinner with friends and show up to discover that Mr. and Mrs. Host are at odds? The angry looks, the subtle snide comments. It's horribly awkward, isn't it?

Your staff will simply enjoy their work more when they see you focusing on wins and when they feel a thread of celebration woven into the workplace. Fun is great for morale and productivity.

2. Your team will risk more and do more.

Risk is scary. Presenting a big idea or pushing past your comfort zone can be stressful and intimidating for your team. It can also be exhilarating. A culture of celebration helps to create an environment where your team can feel free to risk more.

When your team sees you celebrating wins they are more willing to voice bigger ideas and push their boundaries. I see this all the time with new actors on stage. The fear of failing is minimized by the greater desire to win and be celebrated.

A culture of celebration helps you be more open to new ideas, too. Ever have days when you're just mad at the world? We all do. You're quick to poke holes in other people's ideas and you burst bubbles faster than a 5-year-old with bubble wrap. Similar to our discussion on perspective, when you have trained yourself to look for reasons to celebrate others, you will automatically be more receptive to their contributions.

3. Your team will be more open to criticism.

I trust you understand that I'm not asking you to run your entire organization like a brainstorming session where no idea is a bad idea. There are plenty of bad ideas out there. They often start with someone like me saying, "This is going to be funny."

Your team will have bad ideas. You will have bad ideas. Healthy criticism is one of the ways we improve our work and move toward excellence. On the other hand, nothing will stunt your team's growth more than unhealthy or constant criticism.

Remember the leader I mentioned in the chapter on Perspective? The only interaction he had with his team was when they did something wrong. How eager would you be to take his call? I'll bet this type of leader leaves a lot of messages.

What if this leader called you up every time you did something well? What if he occasionally checked in just to thank, encourage and celebrate you? What if he publicly acknowledged appreciation for your work at the next meeting? Would you be more willing to pick up the phone when he called? You bet. Would you be more open to criticism when the time came? I think you would.

Following a Panic Squad show, we always list our favorite parts of the show, and the best lines of the night before we discuss the things we could have improved. We don't start with the negative and point fingers. We celebrate the great show we just performed. We recall great moments. Then we look for ways to make it even better.

When you create a culture of celebration you do not lose your right to challenge ideas and reprimand poor work. I would argue that you have more of an opportunity to challenge your staff because they trust you to also celebrate their wins.

4. Your team will be equipped to deal with disappointment and failure.

Remember the RPS Entourage exercise? Everyone is having a blast shouting and cheering on their team. The thing is, most of them are losing. With each battle half of the players lose until there is only one winner in a room full of losers.

So why is everyone in such a great mood? It's a question I ask in every exercise. "Why are you all so happy? Everyone except Lindsey lost!" I love the answers I get. It's all about team. It's about being part of something bigger.

One woman said in a recent workshop, "My personal failure seemed insignificant in the scope of becoming part of the winning team. I got over my own loss very quickly because I immediately had an opportunity to turn around and cheer for my team."

Amen to that! Celebration softens the blow of disappointment and failure. Celebrating keeps the wins fresh in your mind. This is so helpful when you hit low times.

5. Your team will begin to celebrate each other.

Great leaders begin to see their actions modeled by their team. It's not something they request or enforce. It just happens. We lead by example, and our behavior is duplicated, for better or worse. Become a leader who creates a culture of celebration, and your team will join you. You'll begin to see them encouraging and celebrating one another. They begin to look for ways to see and celebrate the success of their teammates. It's a wonderful thing.

An Invitation To The Party

The "fourth wall" is a theater term used to describe the imaginary wall between the stage and the audience. The rule in theatre is to never break the fourth wall. The story evolving on stage is it's own world. Being distracted by a child in the audience, falling off the stage, and other gaffs break the wall and destroy the magic of the story.

Suddenly, instead of being Sir Lancelot riding through the forest on your noble steed, you are Larry in cardboard armor, grimacing as the kid in row 5 picks his nose and eats it. Breaking the fourth wall can wreck the magic of theater.

Even most improv companies discourage breaking the fourth wall. The goal is to create incredible characters and stories and stick with them. Draw the audience in. Interacting with the audience from within the scene wrecks the magic.

Whatever.

Sure, I see the point. But that's not the way we do it. During a Panic Squad performance, we break the fourth wall all the time. We simply have a different goal that takes precedence over theater rules.

Our goal is to entertain you. We've found that one of the best ways to entertain you is to invite you to our party. Include you in the joke. We perform with you as if you were one of the team. "Thank you for coming to the show, you're one of us now. This is going to be so much fun!"

Of course we work hard at doing great improv comedy. Think back to the chapter on direction and structure and all the work that goes into an excellent performance. We also want you to feel like you're one of us. We do that by giving you a backstage pass from the stage. We do it by breaking the fourth wall and bringing you into the fun.

One thing audiences love is when we celebrate each other. I know some improv teams that talk about how hard it is to stay in character and keep a straight face when another team member lands an awesome joke. We don't even try. We always laugh at each other's jokes. Sometimes we laugh really hard. The audience absolutely loves it.

Other times, when a scene ends we'll call out something great an actor said or did and relive it with the audience for a moment. The audience loves that, too. We laugh together all over again.

Throughout the show our actors will give each other a subtle nod or wink when they deliver a brilliant line or offer a sweet idea to move the scene forward. This keeps us motivated, supported and having fun.

Sometimes it's not so subtle. An actor delivers a great line and the audience dies. As the wave of laughter is beginning to settle, the other actors will walk over, give the guy a fist bump and then take their place in the scene again. The audience usually laughs and applauds all over again.

What are we doing? We're celebrating the small wins. We're celebrating each other. We're inviting the audience to the party to celebrate with us. This creates an incredible environment for an improv show. In a performance that is all about relationship, entertainment and momentum, it's golden.

Become A Bloodhound.

You can become a leader that creates this kind of environment for your team, too. Create a culture or celebration. Don't wait for the curtain to close to let everyone know they did a great job. Celebrate in the moment and throughout the project. It's a great way to keep your team motivated and having fun.

Become a celebration bloodhound. A bloodhound has a phenomenal sense of smell. They are tireless when following a scent and can track a scent for several miles that is several days old. In 1954 a bloodhound tracked and found some people in Oregon 330 hours after they went missing.[18]

Be a leader who hunts for reasons to celebrate and give recognition to your team. It does not have to be big or costly or over the top. It can even just be you voicing how much you appreciate someone. Celebrate them as a team, and as individuals. Do that often.

Don't feel you need to be sneaky about it, either.

"If Bob and Rick hear me congratulating Samantha, they might be envious."

Yes, maybe. Maybe that's just the kick in the caboose that Bob and Rick need. Or, like everybody on The Price is Right, Bob and Rick might start visualizing their name being called next and become motivated.

When your team sees that you are a leader who is looking to celebrate his team, your team will begin looking for ways to win.

Staff Christmas parties are great. But handing Ralph the "Trophy of Awesomeness" to keep on his desk that week is better. Both for Ralph and the rest of the team. Ralph got the trophy this week, but there are still plenty of other chances for others to hear their name called.

Be sure not to only celebrate company achievements. In fact, the more your celebration is connected to a person or specific result, the more powerful the celebration.

There is so much to celebrate in every organization if you are looking for it. Celebrate the small wins, the milestones, the little victories. As a leader, develop a culture of celebration.

Chapter 5: Amazing Performance or Perform Amazingly?

There I was, feet hanging off the end of the twin bed, laying between Star Wars sheets and staring up at a galaxy of glow in the dark stars on the ceiling. I was in a small town in Alberta, Canada. The 10-year-old whose room I had been given to sleep in was staying at a friend's house.

His shaggy dog, the one that usually slept with him, did not go to the friend's house. It whined and scratched at my door. All. Night. Long.

I hoped the others guys were having better luck with their hosts. I remember thinking, "I can't wait to get on the plane tomorrow so I can get some sleep." Not a thought I often have. I remember also thinking, "I can't do this anymore."

By "this", I didn't mean perform improv comedy. I loved my job. I still do. But I could no longer bend so far backwards for a client that it affected my ability to do my job. I could no longer keep making decisions which put my teammates in a position that frustrated them and made them feel devalued.

I wanted so badly to give the client an amazing performance, both on and off the stage, that I was hurting our ability to perform amazingly as a team. I wanted to be easy to work with. I wanted to be accommodating, humble and service-minded.

My problem was I was missing an important truth. A team needs to be healthy and happy if they are to consistently perform great things. As leaders we have to take care of our team. Equip your team to perform amazingly and they will consistently create amazing performances.

Projects will start and end. Clients will come and go. Your team is there for the long haul. If fact, the better you take care of your team the longer they stick around.

Who Do You Love?

Who are you serving? Is it your customers—be it consumers, your congregation, or another business? Or is it your team? The correct answer is both. We all know that. It gets trickier when we're asked who we see as the priority.

It's so easy to put the customers first.

"We aim to deliver exceptional service to our clients and grow profitably as a result."

"The mission of our non-profit is to care for 'XYZ Group'. We are all committed to give time and energy to make that happen."

"As a church we exist to love and serve our congregation and the surrounding community."

These are all great statements. True statements. The problem is that each of the previous statements is describing *what* the team is doing, not *how* it happens. Recall that in chapter one we discovered the importance of learning *how* to lead, not where or what to lead.

Look again at the above statements and ask yourself, "How will this be accomplished?" Try to come up with a good answer that doesn't involve exceptional work by a healthy, motivated team. Your answers may not include a superhero, your fairy godmother, James T. Kirk or The Force. That's cheating.

As a leader, your team must be your priority. You do not lead your customers. You lead and support your team. Then, as a team, you deliver an amazing experience to your customers.

This doesn't mean cater to every complaint or demand your staff throws down. It does mean, however, that you view your team as your most important relationship and resource. Care for them, train them and equip them to succeed.

Jellyfish Don't Have Backbones

In the beginning of our career I wanted to move far away from the "Selfish Jerk Artist" end of things. I had witnessed some bands and artists that completely disrespect the time and effort of their hosts. Calls at 3:00am with ridiculous requests, throwing fits over unimportant details, and general "You are here to serve me" attitudes. I don't ever want to be that performer.

I am truly grateful for the events we get to serve. When you book The Panic Squad, you are telling us you value our ability as performers, and you're enabling us to do what we love and feed our families. That's big, and we appreciate it.

We also understand that you have put an incredible amount of time into organizing and promoting your event. You are trusting us to partner with you in making it a success. We're here to serve you. I mean that, but sometimes that attitude gets me into trouble.

I tend to swing too far the other way sometimes. I've already disclosed that I struggle with being a people pleaser. I fight the feeling that I'm asking too much or being a hassle.

I so fear being viewed as a jerk artist that at times I have found myself in the jellyfish camp. Jellyfish don't have backbones. That's not healthy either. There has to be balance. Yes, it's important to be humble, grateful and to treat others with respect. There are also times when you need to stand up for yourself and your team so you can do your job well.

I wanted so badly to serve my clients that I was willing to sacrifice basic comfort, for myself and for my team, so we wouldn't appear arrogant and demanding.

This is backwards when you think about it. What event organizer has ever said the following?

"They looked tired, weren't very funny, and smelled like a big shaggy dog. But we saved money on accommodations. Let's book them again!"

I'm willing to bet most event organizers would rather say something like this.

"That was incredible! A little more than we were hoping to spend, but WOW. Everyone is still talking about the show. Let's bring them back next year."

Yep, that's more like it, isn't it?

Leading For The Long Haul

Making sure that your team is healthy and cared for sets them up to perform amazingly, and to do it consistently. That's why every serious performer or speaker has a rider.

A rider is simply a document that lists what an artist needs to do their job well. It covers everything from technical needs on stage to information on meals, travel and hotels. Our rider is pretty simple. In fact clients often mention how easy we are to host. More like pet rocks than rock bands.

Other riders are not so simple. I've seen riders that are longer than this book. Seriously. We've been at events with an artist who only eats meals on real china. "Don't you serve me on that cheap ceramic, boy!" I'm not judging, but that's not me, either.

While The Panic Squad Rider is very simple, it has more backbone than it did in the beginning. Over the years I've gotten better at finding a balance between humility and the ability to do our job well. Our performance rider has evolved with me.

We normally perform in teams of three and we used to all cram into one room to save the client money. Someone always got the hotel's prison cot. We had different games we'd play and the loser got the cot. That person never slept well. That's why we had to create a mercy rule. Even if you had a streak of bad luck in the games, you never had to take the cot more than three times in a row.

We also used to never question billeting (staying in someone's home) either. We were happy to be serving you and would be grateful for whatever accommodations you gave us.

That attitude landed me between Star Wars sheets in a 10-year-old's bedroom that smelled like his dog.

It landed us all in a youth pastor's hot, messy bachelor pad in Florida. We slept on the floor and his couch. One of my actors forgot to move his backpack off of the floor and the guy's dogs chewed it up. The guy said, "I warned you, man! They chew everything!"

He offered us hot dog wieners and granola bars for breakfast.

It's kind of funny that both of these stories involve dogs. Did I mention I'm allergic to pets? Yep. That's in the rider now, too. I don't have anything against pets. I just find that I perform better comedy when I'm not wheezing and trying to see out of swollen eyes.

"What's wrong with him? He looks like Will Smith in the movie, Hitch. [19] Do you hear his breathing? I think he's dying. "

"He'll be fine. Did I mention we saved money by not booking hotel rooms?"

Not all of our billeting experiences have been bad. Some have been fine. Some have been incredible. We stayed with an NHL player in North Carolina, and it was a fabulous experience. We had our own rooms and got a good night sleep. We swam in the pool, we had a Nerf gun war with his kids and we got to know a great family. It was a wonderful experience.

That's why there is some flexible language in our rider. Here are the rules. If you have a different idea, let's talk.

I protect myself and my team from tough situations with some simple rules created to give the customer a better performance. Sometimes our rider isn't read or the client simply doesn't care, and we find ourselves in a tough spot. That's when it's my job as the leader to hold the line.

Sometimes When You Lose, You Win

I know I have lost at least one client due to standing up for my team and pushing on some items we needed changed so we could create an excellent experience for the event. What I lost in business from that client has been replaced ten fold in the trust and respect of my teammates. It's been a process where I have had to do a lot of growing. I had to do some apologizing to my team, find a backbone and make some changes over the years. But my relationship with my team has really grown from it.

Even with our evolved rider that keeps us out of prison cots and asks for more than hot dog wieners and granola bars, we're still one of the easiest acts to work with out there today. That feels good. You know what else? We are a team that consistently performs amazingly together. A by-product of which is...you guessed it...Amazing Performances.

How About You?

You're probably not a touring entertainer like I am. I doubt you have a rider like I do. But I'll bet there are times you struggle with putting your work and mission before your team.

This usually stems from something very positive, dedication. You're a leader. You are wholly invested in your business, church or organization. You dream, you worry, and you work hard. You dream that this will be better than you ever imagined. You worry that it might all crumble or slip away. The dreams and the fears may cause you to focus on the project or the mission more than the people that will help you get there.

Whether you lead a team of improv comedy actors, pastor a church or run the company that wraps that impossible-to-open-cellophane around CDs and DVDS, you must care for your team. You may not have a rider, but there are likely things your team needs that you're not giving them.

There may be ways you like things done that are not the most efficient or effective for your team. There might be rules that make sense to you but hinder your staff's ability to do great work for you. There could be tools or equipment they need that you haven't provided.

What are some ways you need to begin to stand up for your team? How can you show the people you trust to do great work, that they can trust you to lead them to greatness?

A Penny For Your Thoughts...and Your Service

I love a story my friend Scott tells regarding his time working as a server for a fancy restaurant. A group came in, and Scott waited on them. They were demanding and really kept him moving. The restaurant owner noted how hard Scott was working and she encouraged him to keep up his excellent service. At the end of the dinner Scott delivered a sizable bill and thanked the party for coming.

When they finally left the table, Scott and the owner both went over, anticipating a nice tip. There was only change on the table. Nothing on the credit card slip, either. Scott was astonished and disappointed. That's when the owner scooped up the change and went after them.

She caught up with the party just outside of the restaurant. She confronted the gentleman who had paid the bill, took his hand, put the change back into his palm and declared, "If this is all you think that service was worth then you can keep it. It's an insult."

Scott, who was standing in the doorway, was shocked. He felt respected, valued, and vindicated. His own desire to serve that owner soared. I'm sure the restaurant lost some customers that evening. I doubt the offending party ever returned. I also believe the owner knew that her team's ability to deliver excellent food and service would keep tables full anyway. She was right.

She chose her team over the customer. You and I both know that story was retold to every server, hostess, chef and dishwasher at that restaurant. Her customers continued to come and go, and her loyal, valued staff continued to serve them with excellence.

Bi-Polar Leadership

Sometimes it's not a client issue, outdated equipment or a lack of training that is hindering our team. Sometimes it's the leader. Sometimes we create a negative view of our team that isn't true.

I joke with my actors that there are times I view them with the split personalities of Gollom and Sméagol from The Lord Of The Rings, The Two Towers.[20]

Gollum: "Nasty, greedy performers. They wants too much. They takes advantage of us."

Sméagol: "No, no they's our friends. They loves us. They works hard for us."

Gollum: "Tricksy performers. They don't understand how easy they haves it."

Sméagol: "They wants to be excellent, we must help them. We must lead them."

Do you ever find yourself suffering from bi-polar leadership? One day you think the world of your team and feel lucky to be working alongside such a stellar group. The next day you feel like they don't work hard enough, they aren't committed enough and just don't get it.

Part of the reason might be the week you're having. You're stressed out, tired and no one understands the pressure you're under. When you're mad at your team, it's smart to ask yourself, "Am I being consistent? Would I still feel this way if my personal circumstances were different, if I was less stressed or more rested?"

Perspective is important, too. You are seeing things from your viewpoint. Your team is seeing the situation from their perspective. They are not the same.

Think back to a time before you were a leader. Did you always understand why your leader made the decisions he did? Did you ever feel ignored or undervalued? Could it be that your team is feeling the same way?

Am I Crystal Clear?

Whenever I start to go into Gollum mode, I try to look at things from my actor's perspective. Have I been clear in my communication with them? Do they understand the big picture and why I've done this or that? What are some concerns they might have? Would I be feeling the same if I were in their shoes?

Sometimes I discover there are some changes I need to make. Other times I find that I have made the right decision but may not have been clear in communicating why it is the best decision. There are also times when my actors are simply being hard to deal with. That's a possibility, too.

It's All About The Relationship

Teamwork is everything in improv. As we've already discussed in this book, improv is the epitome of unscripted work. We are creating in the moment. We become experts in learning how to work together in any situation so that the situation doesn't matter.

You want us to do a scene about an ostrich mafia? We've got it. You shout out "slug racing" when we ask for a unique sport? No problem. We'll have you believing we've been in the slug-racing game for years.

When we mess up in improv, it is almost never due to the details of the scene. When a scene bombs, it's because the relationship has failed. Someone wasn't listening and missed an important offer. An actor felt unsupported and stopped supporting others. Or the actors brought off-stage conflict with them into the scene.

As a professional entertainer, I've had to push through all kinds of hardships on stage. I've performed when I'm exhausted, when I'm sick, with a sprained ankle, with a patch over one eye and with my arm in a cast. I've had to continue a show after getting hit in the face by a size 11 Birkenstock sandal. The hardest shows, however, have been when I'm not getting along with my team.

The times we have taken the stage angry at each other have been the toughest. It's hard to do great improv when you don't want to support the person next to you. I'm more hesitant to offer creative ideas when I don't trust my teammate to support them. When an improv show is corrupted by dueling egos, it's going to be rough.

We have also noticed that our best shows, the really memorable ones, have been when we're having a great time together as actors. Great relationships make for great performances. When we are laughing with one another before taking the stage, it's going to be an incredible show.

Reality Is A Real Pain

I wish that every show were like that. But real life says that we are not always going to be excited to be around each other. Roads have potholes. Seagulls poop while flying. Relationships aren't perfect. That's life.

Fortunately, that doesn't mean the relationship has to suffer. At an event in Kansas City one of the other actors and I really got into it over something. We were both really mad, and we were on in 5 minutes.

We took a breath, agreed that we still needed to work this out. We said that we trusted and respected each other and were looking forward to putting this issue to rest. Then we prayed together, hugged it out and took the stage. We nailed the performance.

Three things were true.

1. We were both mad and had an unresolved issue we still needed to work through.

2. We really did trust and respect each other. The issue didn't affect the relationship.

3. We were professionals and had a job to do.

The health of our relationship allowed us to hit some potholes without breaking down. Our perspective was based in truth. We had a common goal, to nail the performance, and knew we needed to support each other to accomplish that.

Become a leader who intentionally fosters a good relationship with, and within, your team. Create a great relationship now so you can succeed in the moment. Even in times when the moment has presented a tough situation.

The Proper Care and Feeding of Teams

My 5-year-old is getting a newt for his birthday. He's so excited. We set up the tank and he carefully placed all the stuff inside. He kept saying things like, "my newt will like this rock here." Or, "the newt will like looking at this plant over here." As if the newt cares. "Just give me some more of them bloodworms!" say most newts. But it's precious nonetheless.

My son has no idea how to care for a newt. He wants to play with the newt like you might play with a dog. He wants to sleep with it and take a bath with it. He wants to walk around with the newt on his shoulder like a parakeet.

He was devastated when I told him you aren't really supposed to handle them that much.

"He can't take a bath with you because the chlorine in the water will hurt the newt."

"He can't have a bite of your hamburger. You'll have to feel him newt pellets or worm cubes."

"No, you can't eat the newt pellets or worm cubes, either."

Now he gets it, but there was a learning curve. He won't be sharing a burger with the newt, but he knows how to care for it and keep it happy and healthy now. The newt's name is going to be Mike, by the way. My son decided to name him Mike Newton Bright. Good name for a newt.

As leaders we can tend to see our teams like my son viewed his prospective newt. We have big ideas about how great our team will be and the wonderful things we'll do together. Then we realize that our team is made up of different people with unique gifts, flaws, needs and personalities and we're not sure what to do with them.

Allow me to share some ideas with you.

Here Are 5 Ways We Care For Each Other In Improv, and How You Can Use Them To Care For Your Team, Too.

1. Be Present

For improv to work, everyone in the scene and on the sidelines has to be present. This means they are engaged with what is happening in the scene. They know what has already happened, what is going on now and what needs to happen next to move the scene forward.

When you are present, you hear offers. Let's say an actor is sitting outside of the scene when a character in the scene says, "Mr. Jenkins should be here any minute with our cheese delivery." An actor who is present hears that offer and is ready to come in as Mr. Jenkins. He also knows what else has been said about Mr. Jenkins earlier in the scene.

How awkward would it be for the actor on the sidelines be playing with his phone or thinking about how great he was in the last scene? He misses the offer but the audience doesn't. The scene stalls and that actor looks like an idiot.

When you're not present in improv you look foolish, you miss offers and you communicate to the other actors that you're not supporting their work. When an actor is present in a scene, she looks brilliant, she hears offers, and communicates to the other actors that she values their ideas.

Listen well

How can you be present as a leader? First, know what's going on. Read the reports and emails your team sends you. Don't be the leader that says, "Oh, did you send me that? I haven't had a chance to look at it yet," especially when it is something you asked for.

Listen well. There is a difference between listening to what someone is saying and waiting patiently for your turn to talk. Hearing is not the same as listening. Give a person your attention. Put down your phone and make eye contact. Ask follow-up questions to get more clarity.

Two things happen when you do this. First, you hear offers. Maybe you hear a great idea or an opportunity to guide and teach a team member. Second, you demonstrate to your team that you value their contribution. I cannot think of a better way to show your team you value them than to truly listen to them.

There is nothing more frustrating for your team than a leader who doesn't listen. I had coffee last month with a gentleman who was terribly frustrated with his job. His number one complaint? Leadership doesn't listen. It didn't matter how much time, research or energy went into his ideas, he simply wasn't heard. It was crushing his confidence and desire to contribute, and he is looking for other employment.

Eye hate it when he does that

My friend Tim used to act with The Panic Squad and is now in Los Angeles doing TV and film. Tim has this infuriating gimmick that I both hated and loved. When Tim would listen to you, he would nod and agree verbally, but he would look just to the side of your eyes, usually at one of your ears. It was eye contact but not really. Something was obviously a little off.

I hated when Tim did this to me but loved watching him do it to others. You can't have a serious conversation with Tim when he does this. It is so unnerving and distracting. It was hilarious to see others become more and more uncomfortable as they tried to talk with Tim. It also demonstrates the importance of being completely present when communicating with your team. Are you giving them your undivided attention, or just mostly listening?

Finally, a great way to be present as a leader is to have a finger on the pulse of your team's life outside of work. Do they have family? When is their birthday or anniversary? What are some passions they have outside the office? Rock climbing, chess tournaments, hamster racing? Become a leader who is present in these areas of their lives and you will demonstrate that you care for your team.

2. Listen Then Act

Remember improv's "Yes And" principle? You agree with someone's offer then contribute your own. This is how we move forward.

I think a lot of leaders miss the "And" piece with their team. Some leaders are good listeners, but they are horrible at follow-up. Nothing says, "I don't really care" like dropping someone else's important idea or concern. To you, it may be just one more thing on a list of one hundred important things you have to do as a leader. To your staff member, it may feel like the most important thing ever.

I'm not saying that you have to meet every request or idea with a "Yes" answer. I'm saying the "Yes" is listening to the idea, then the "And" is your movement on the idea. It's the follow-up. It means when you say you are going to think about it and get back to them, you actually do. I think most employees would rather have you come back with a "no," along with some reasoning and direction than receive no answer at all.

A non-answer shouts loudly, "You and your idea are not worth another second of my time!" Of course you don't feel that way. Then why would you communicate that sentiment by neglecting to take action and get back to them with an answer?

Listening to your team shows you value them. Acting on what you hear and committing to follow-up increases that value exponentially. On the other hand, a lack of response erases any credibility you gained by listening.

"Yes (listening) But (no action) I'm not really going to do anything with that."

3. The Call Back

A call back is simply bringing a successful joke back in a different way. This is an age-old strategy in comedy and is used in stand-up, sketches and improv.

Stand-up and sketch comedians write it into their scripts. Improv actors listen for great ideas and bank them for later in the scene or show.

The call back is a wonderful tool for a few reasons. It's already been successful once. The audience has already told you, "We like that line!"

It relates even more the second time. The best comedy relates in the most ways to the audience. Airplane jokes are funnier to people who travel often. With a call back, everyone in the audience was there the first time the joke hit. Now they are on the inside of an inside joke. People love that feeling.

Finally, in improv, when an actor brings back a joke another actor used earlier it's like giving them a giant high-five in front of everyone. You are essentially saying, "That was brilliant!" You are celebrating the success of another actor's great idea. The audience catches that and they love it.

Become a leader who uses call backs. Please don't start to do stand-up in your staff meetings. Chances are you're horrible at it. What I mean is acknowledge your team's great ideas in front of everyone.

"Sara and I were talking yesterday and she had a great idea to give back to the community."

"Remember when Nathan suggested we hire The Panic Squad for our volunteer appreciation event? Let's talk some more about that."

"Jennifer showed me some amazing research she put together that I think you all should see."

"José, will you tell the rest of the group about your idea for increasing traffic to our website? The whole team needs to hear this."

As a leader, you are using call backs when you take a team contribution that you appreciate and bring it back into focus for the entire team. The results are similar to the benefits of a call back in comedy.

You bring a successful idea back to the table. You are bringing the rest of the team into the process and giving them a chance to support and enjoy good work. You are highlighting what good work looks like for your team. Best of all, you are giving that person a giant high-five in front of everyone. Want to see more ideas and effort coming from your team? Use call backs as a leader.

4. Ask For Their Help

Remember Patrick Lencioni's thoughts on supporting your team by genuinely asking for their help?

As I stated in chapter one, asking your team for help is not weakness; it's leadership. It's the strength to see you are not capable of doing something as well as someone else on your team. It's the humility to ask for help. It's the awareness to offer your team an opportunity to grow through leading you.

Look for qualities you admire in people on your team that coincide with areas where you need improvement. Then ask them to help you. This is a great way to be present. It demonstrates that you are both in tune with their unique abilities and with your own need for growth and improvement in some areas.

5. Training and Equipping

What are your team's needs? Do you value your team enough to give them the tools and training they need to be excellent? A great way to show your team you value their work is to use company time and resources to help them grow.

The Panic Squad has done some great training over the years. Early in our career we hired veteran actors from professional TheatreSports leagues to come out and workshop our craft. We would hire improv instructors to attend one of our shows and give us a thorough critique and notes. Later, as we grew as entertainers, we attended master level workshops with improv greats like Keith Johnstone.

The different trainings and critiques we have been a part of have taught us some invaluable lessons. Training has helped us hone our craft and turned us into the excellent improv team we are today.

Give your team opportunities to learn and grow. Invest time and resources into training that will teach new skills and strategies. Developing your team is a great way to show you are in tune with their needs and care about their contribution to your mission and organization.

You Can Do This

Being a leader is difficult. You have a lot on your plate, but so does your team. They believe in what you are creating together and want to be excellent for you. Become a leader who doesn't get caught up in an amazing performance for your customer to the detriment of your team. Become a leader who equips your team to perform amazingly so together you can consistently create amazing performances.

Chapter 6: The Secret Sauce – How To Really Win In Improv and Leadership

It's the last scene of the night. Dann, Elijah and I have performed a great show and we have the audience right where we want them. They can't wait to see what we're going to do next.

Elijah looks at me and gives me a quick, upward tilt of his chin. Without saying a word he has essentially said, "I've got this. Follow my lead."

Elijah sets up some chairs and then says, "Alright, let's see who the next appointment is for couples counseling. Ah yes, John and Suzanne."

I immediately turn to Dann and say, "I'll be John." You have to be quick in improv. The early bird gets to play the man. The crowd laughs as Dann throws his hands in the air in exasperation. They love it when we put each other on the spot.

Dann and I enter the scene as John and Suzanne and take our seats in the counseling office. Elijah asks me to explain the problems I am having with Suzanne. I tell him that she doesn't give me attention anymore, not since she discovered her new hobby.

Then I walk to the front of the stage. "What is Suzanne's new hobby?" I ask the audience. The crowd begins to shout out ideas, and I go with knitting sweaters from belly button lint. Pure gold.

Then Suzanne is asked to respond. Dann, aka Suzanne, says that she had to find a new hobby because I'm never around anymore. I spend all my time at my new job. Dann goes to the audience for my new job and comes back with Squid Wrangler.

Perfect. It's going to be a great scene. That's when Elijah drops the bomb on us. He casually walks over to the grand piano that is on the corner of the church's stage, and sits down. I begin to sweat a little.

"Welcome to musical therapy," he says, "where we work out our issues through song." Dann and my mouths drop open. The audience roars and applauds. I sweat a little more. Elijah is an incredible musician. Dann can sing just fine. We discussed my musical ability in chapter one.

"Ladies first," I say to my wife, Suzanne. The audience chuckles. I got him again. That's twice now.

Dann quickly comes back with, "No dear, I want to submit to your leadership. You go first." Oh man, that was brilliant. We're performing at a marriage conference. He has me. The crowd loves it. Elijah comes over and fist bumps Dann. The crowd laughs again and applauds Dann as I hang my head.

I walk to the front of the stage as Elijah begins a soft, slow melody. I stare him down. "Seriously? A love ballad?"

"Yep," he responds, "a love ballad about your wife knitting sweaters from bellybutton lint." Then he and

Dann both crack up, along with the crowd. Oh brother. Here we go…

Elijah plays a note and hums for me as I try to find the right key to sing in. I wish I were a janitor because then I would have more keys. Apparently the one key I have doesn't fit the song, because it definitely isn't unlocking any hidden musical talent.

Oh well, I push forward. The singing is bad, but I nail some great lines and pull off some decent rhymes. The song is actually quite funny. When I finish the ballad I end up getting some incredible applause.

A Genuine Failure

Why the applause and cheers? The song was unpolished and off-key. You wouldn't applaud Céline Dion if she sang off-key. Well, not unless you're Canadian, then she can do no wrong in your eyes. Most of us, however, would not be pleased with an off-key Céline. So why am I getting applause?

It all comes down to authenticity.

Audiences love the authenticity and vulnerability of improv. They love the spontaneity, the risk and even the rough edges. Remember, improv is the high wire act of comedy.

The crowd applauds my song because they understand the agreement. They just asked me to sing a song about my wife knitting sweaters from belly-button lint and how that impacts our marriage.

It's obvious that I'm uncomfortable singing. The audience can't wait to see what happens. They wonder if I'm really going to go for it and how I'm going to pull it off.

The actors know the deal, too. We know the audience wants desperately to see what happens next. We know they're more interested in whether or not we will jump in with both feet than if we will be polished and perfect.

So I go for it with everything I've got. Not fearing failure. Because failing may be just as entertaining, and we're entertainers.

Truth Be Told

The truth is I know Elijah is going to make me sing. We talked about it ahead of time. I have no idea what the scene or the song will be about, but I know it's coming. We play it up for the pure entertainment of the audience.

Well, we partly play it up. My fear is real. Every single time I have to sing on stage I'm terrified. It is incredibly uncomfortable for me. The reason I push on past that fear is because I know how much it means to the audience.

I know they love improv for what it is—risky and unpredictable. I know the audience will extend grace to me if I'm willing to be authentic and vulnerable with them. It's a beautiful relationship. When I'm on stage in front of a warm audience and grace is in play, I can do anything.

Both the actors and the audience understand that the only real failure is shutting down and not trying. It's saying no, and refusing to move forward.

Imagine if I gave the audience a number of reasons for why they would not want to hear me sing, then sat down. Done. Leave the singing to someone more qualified.

It would be a huge let down. I would destroy my credibility with the audience and damage the trust of my teammates. I would probably get booed.

How About You?

What happens when you refuse to lead with authenticity? You probably won't get booed by your staff. Well, at least not to your face. Nonetheless, being real and vulnerable is just as important in leadership as it is in improv.

I know what you're thinking, "Here we go again." Authenticity is one of those leadership buzz words that finds its way into nearly every blog post, book and podcast these days. It's like the song "Let it go," from Disney's *Frozen*[21] It's catchy but you groan a little every time you hear it now.

I almost did let it go. I seriously considered removing this chapter from the book, simply because of how often others write about being an authentic leader. I considered omitting it, but I couldn't. It's a central part of improv and leadership. It's why improv is loved as an art form. It's how leaders can truly lead well.

Imagine chocolate chip cookies without chocolate chips. How do you feel about hot wings without any heat? Would you like to know a great way to exfoliate your entire body? Go waterskiing without the water.

I recognize that a lot has been said about authenticity. I also tried to imagine a book on improv and leadership without a piece on authenticity. It made about as much sense as waterskiing without water.

Home Crowd Advantage

When I am training people in how to communicate from the stage, one of the things I help them understand is that the audience is on their side. How often do you go to a concert, comedy show, or to hear an expert speak and think to yourself, "I hope this is horrible. I could really use a nap."

In the same way, your team truly wants you to succeed. I hope there is no one in your company that thinks to themselves, "I hope he is a horrible leader, the last thing I want to do is grow in my career, find meaning and be inspired to do great work."

Your team wants you to lead well. They are secretly cheering for you and hoping you will be someone who has what it takes to move this organization forward. They hope you will create an environment where their team can thrive and show them all how to be a part of something great.

One of the keys is authenticity.

Dogs Can Smell Fear, People Can Smell Fake

More evidence for the value of authenticity is found in how people view things that are not genuine. Most people don't have much fondness for the idea of lip syncing pop stars, counterfeit money or hypocritical religious leaders. Our culture is full of fake. With easy access to Photoshop and phrases like, "Well the internet says..." How do we know what's real anymore?

That's one reason I believe people are craving authenticity. In his book, *Lasting Impact – 7 Powerful Conversations The Will Help Your Church Grow*, pastor and leadership expert Carey Nieuwhof suggests that one reason young adults may be walking away from church is an underlying lack of authenticity within the church. He says, "Quite simply, authentic resonates. More than ever people are looking for what's real, what's true and what's authentic."[22]

I agree. People want substance.

We're Not Fooling Anyone

One thing I've learned in 20 years of performing is that audiences are much smarter than we give them credit for. When you are performing or speaking, you have 100 things going on in your mind. You're thinking about your material, the timing, how the audience is responding, whether or not you should cut that story. Does that guy just have to use the bathroom or is he leaving? Why does the woman in row three look angry?

The audience, on the other hand, is simply watching and listening. They can sense when you're scared and whether or not you like them. The audience is on your side and wants you to succeed until you demonstrate that you're not on their side. That's when they turn on you.

If I refused to sing about my wife's belly button lint knitting hobby, and instead said I was going to leave the music to the guys who can sing, the audience would see right through me. They would see fear and ego working together. "I'm scared and you're not worth the risk." The audience would feel underappreciated and ripped off.

The Leader In The Mirror

When, as a leader in your organization, you refuse to be authentic and vulnerable with your team they see it for what it is. Fear and ego. They feel ripped off.

You can find all sorts of other ways to describe your resistance to leading with authenticity and transparency. Ways that are less harsh and paint you in a better light. You can point at other leaders above you or the dysfunction of your company. I'll bet though, that if you dig deep enough and are honest with yourself, it will boil down to fear and ego.

You fear that the curtain will be pulled aside and you, the great Leader of Oz, will be revealed as less than everyone thought you were. Somewhere, whether consciously or not, you have decided your team and your organization are not worth that risk.

I say risk it. I say trust that grace is in play and that your team is on your side. They are not interested in whether or not you are polished and perfect. They are more interested in whether or not you will move forward in spite of your fears and take them with you.

The reason that audiences love the imperfection of improv is because everyone in the room identifies with the actors on some level. I see it in their eyes. They are scared for us and with us. They celebrate for us and with us. Imperfect people living imperfect lives identify with the authenticity and vulnerability of an improv show. In the same moment they are excited to be a part of the show and relieved they are not on stage with us.

Could it be that this is how your team sees you? Is it possible that the unique individuals God has given you the privilege of leading are simply imperfect people looking to identify with and be led by you? They are, at the same time, excited to be a part of your team and relieved that you are the one leading.

Is it possible that by being authentic, vulnerable and transparent you become a leader who resonates with the imperfect people on your team and inspires them to do great work? I think that's very possible

Here Are 5 Ways To Become An Incredibly Authentic and Effective Leader.

1. See Failure For What It Is

Failure. An idea flops, a project tanks, a joke bombs. It happens to all of us. In improv it happens all the time. It's the nature of unscripted comedy. Your work is unscripted, too. So failure is going to undoubtedly come your way from time to time.

As a leader, train yourself and your team to see failure for what it really is, the merciful end to a bad idea or wrong path and the opportunity to start over with more information and a keener sense of direction.

I've had some spectacular failures in my personal life, in business and onstage.

On my first date I wrecked my dad's car and covered my date in cow manure. Seriously. There was not a second date.

In my first year of marriage, my wife was out of town on a missions trip. I arranged for my mother to come over and clean our house as a gift to my wife. The sad thing is there are a number of men reading this who see nothing wrong with that idea. What woman wouldn't want their mother-in-law to come over and clean their house for them?

All women on earth, that's who. Luckily, I was bragging about this plan to some ladies at work. They let me know in no uncertain terms that it was a horrible idea. I called my mom and canceled. I thought I had dodged a bullet but I still got in trouble. My wife was mad that I had even considered the idea.

Extra! Extra! Read all about it!

We've failed in our career, too. Every professional entertainer has horror stories of gigs gone wrong and moments on stage you'd give anything to take back. We decided to share ours with the world.

Every business has a page of testimonials where happy clients say nice things about their work. The Panic Squad does too. We're very proud of our excellent track record. Our page is called, "Successful Missions."[23]

We also have a page titled, "Failed Missions".[24] As far as I know, we're the only company that does this. The page lists our worst failures. As awkward or horrible as they were at the time, we can laugh at them now and hope others will too.

Each of our failures was also a learning experience that made us better comedians in the end. That's why we also list what we learned from each fiasco, and what we changed to ensure it never happened again.

We get a lot of positive comments regarding our failed missions page. One client in Georgia even booked us because of what he read there. He told me it gave him confidence that we would do a great job at his event. Imagine that, a page listing our worst failures and what we learned from them ends up inspiring a new client to book us. By the way, he was right. We crushed it at his event. He was thrilled.

Become a leader who calls failure what it is. An opportunity to change and grow.

2. Be Vulnerable

Vulnerability is more about trust than anything else. Do you trust your team to follow and support the real you? Remember, trust is essential in improv. The day an improv actor becomes fearless on stage is the day he learns to trust his team to support his ideas and trusts the audience to extend grace if the idea flops.

In his bestselling book, *The Advantage – Why Organizational Health Trumps Everything Else in Business,* Patrick Lencioni gives a great description of the type of trust needed to build a great team. He calls it vulnerability-based trust, and defines it as the type of trust that is created when team members become comfortable being completely transparent with one another. Some examples he gives are the ability to genuinely say, "I screwed up", or "I need help," or "Your idea is better than mine."[25]

Lencioni goes on to say, "At the heart of vulnerability lies the willingness of people to abandon their pride and their fear, to sacrifice their egos for the collective good of the team."[26] Wow, sounds a lot like improv, doesn't it?

He continues, "While this can be a little threatening and uncomfortable at first, ultimately it becomes liberating for people who are tired of spending time and energy overthinking their actions and managing interpersonal politics at work."[27]

I would gladly perform improv with Patrick Lencioni any day.

You can become a leader who is comfortable being vulnerable with your team. Your tendency will be to think that admitting your own shortcomings will somehow lessen your team's view of your ability to lead. I doubt it. More often it says to your team, "I'm like you. We're the same. I hope to overcome my hurdles just like you hope to overcome your own."

The authenticity of admitting you don't have it all together frees you to learn from your mistakes alongside your team. Take a cue from improv comedy. Allow your leadership to resonate with imperfect people working in an unscripted workplace.

3. Embrace Conflict

We have a saying in improv, "Get into trouble." Every scene needs a good conflict. No audience wants to watch two actors stand around and discuss the weather. Get into trouble then make it worse. Now you've got something worth watching. Now the audience is truly engaged.

Leadership is the same way. If you want your team to do great work, you have to be a leader who doesn't mind trouble. Too often a leader takes the role of keeping the peace, making sure everything is running smoothly and no one is getting their toes stepped on. Then they ask where the passion is from their team.

Well Bob Barker, if you weren't constantly asking everyone to spay and neuter their pets, maybe you would see some passion now and then.

Be a leader who embraces healthy conflict rather than shuts it down. Don't be afraid of heated discussion and diverse ideas. When you see that a team member is taking issue with an idea, mine for truth. Dig deeper in a caring and respectful manner. Facilitating healthy conflict will get to the root of your team's best ideas and biggest fears. Healthy conflict is fueled by passion and conviction. When aired in the context of trust and respect, it can be powerful and meaningful.

Just beware of unhealthy conflict for the sake of conflict alone. In improv, we use conflict to engage the audience and move the scene forward. If conflict within your team is outside the structure of trust and respect and if addressing the conflict isn't somehow moving a project or relationship forward, then put an end to it.

There may be some on your team who are confrontational by nature. They like to fight for the sake of fighting. Maybe their motive is to make another team member look bad. When conflict is driven by envy or malice it divides rather than engages. It stalls momentum rather than moves things in the right direction. Don't stand for that.

4. Be Specific

One of the main rules in improv is that every actor is expected to contribute to the scene. It's called, "No Wimping." You are expected to offer ideas. When you wimp in improv, you refuse to make a specific choice.

Wimping is fear based. The less you define something, the less risky it is. A huge fear for novice actors is, "What if my idea is lame?" So when they offer ideas, they become wimps.

Here's a simple example of two wimps doing an improv scene.

"Hi you."

"Hello back."

"I brought you this." (hands something to the other actor)

"Thanks. I'll put that over here."

BORING!

Both actors were worried their ideas would not be received well so they played it safe. They didn't really define anything. Less definition is less risky. It is also really boring and difficult to support.

Here's the same scene again. This time the actors will make specific choices to define their ideas rather than wimp.

"Hi Cousin Zeke! Happy Birthday!"

"Why Hello Cousin Hank! I thought you was still in jail."

"Just escaped this morning. I brought you an orange jumpsuit for your birthday!"

"Thanks! I'll hang it on this wall peg next to my newly framed Bounty Hunter license."

Which scene would you rather see continue?

Become a leader who has the courage to be specific. When you set goals and assign tasks, don't be afraid to define them. Telling your team that you want to improve sales this quarter is a safe request. Telling your team that you want to see Ben create a 7% growth in digital sales and Naomi to find at least 5 new accounts this month is specific. It's riskier and maybe more scary for Ben and Naomi, but it's also a lot easier for them to understand and go after.

Another area where it pays to be specific is consequences. What happens when people are consistently late, disrespectful in meetings or lazy? The safe leader is all about understanding. "Hey, we all have our hiccups. I'm sure it won't happen again."

When a leader is not specific and consistent in discipline, they erode their own respect with the rest of the staff and stunt the offending party's ability to change and grow.

I was fired from my first two jobs following university. I was confident, great with people and interviewed well, but I didn't know how to work. Each time I got canned I was given a reason. This gave me the opportunity to make changes and grow. I'm so thankful my leaders didn't just bury me in unimportant work and leave me alone.

Don't be a wimp. Real leaders make specific choices and tough decisions.

5. Integrity

I'll never forget the day I lied in a job interview. Things were going great. I was answering questions well, and the president of the company seemed impressed.

He asked me to describe some of the most creative ideas I had come up with in my other marketing jobs. For some reason I blanked. Then I heard myself telling the guy about some great ideas, except they weren't my ideas. They were campaigns someone else had told me about long ago. I was telling it like I had come up with the ideas on my own.

It worked. They loved it. The president said that I pretty much had the job. I just needed to come in one more time the next day to meet the owner and finalize things.

As I drove home I tried to be excited. I had just landed a dream job. I would become the marketing manager for an outdoor adventure company. High on the cool factor and right up my alley. So why did I feel so horrible?

My stomach churned. I couldn't eat. I couldn't sleep that night. I had sacrificed my integrity, and it was eating me alive. I prayed for forgiveness and made the decision to make it right. The next day I walked into the meeting where I was supposed to accept the job and confessed instead.

I admitted that I had blanked, and in my fear I had lied. I apologized for being dishonest and said I would understand if they changed their mind on hiring me.

They did. I lost the job. I had really blown it.

On the drive home I couldn't stop smiling. Did you catch that? I was overwhelmed with a sense of peace, joy and gratitude. It felt so right to be myself again. Having my integrity restored was well worth the pain and embarrassment of confessing and losing my dream job. I felt whole again.

Here's the funny, unexpected and ironic ending to the story. A few weeks later the owner of that company was arrested...for fraud. He had been lying to investors, creditors, vendors and pretty much everyone else about his company's finances. When I think about it, I don't know why he didn't give me the job on the spot when I confessed. I was young, creative and willing to lie. A perfect fit for his operation!

Joking aside, what would have become of me had I not confessed and rescued my integrity? Would I ever have been able to take joy in my accomplishments at that company, knowing I had lied to get the job? What if the owner had not been caught and arrested? Who would I have become under the mentorship of a fraudulent owner, having begun my career by lying myself?

Who Will You Become?

If you are a leader, then by definition people are following. You have talented hearts, souls and minds that are following your lead. Be someone worth following.

There is nothing more valuable to a leader than their sense of integrity and self-worth. With your integrity in tact, you are invincible in all the right areas. You may be met with storms, but peace runs deep.

On the other hand, when you have sacrificed your integrity, there is no victory or accolade that will fill the void or ease the turmoil.

I know. I've been on both sides. I also know it's never too late to make things right, be it a day, a month or ten years. If you have sacrificed your own integrity I implore you to do what it takes to make it right. It will be difficult and painful. It will be worth it.

If you are to lead a team to do great work using trust, respect and forward momentum, you have to first trust and respect yourself. You have to clear out the cobwebs and skeletons that are impeding your own ability to move forward.

IMPROV[e] LEADERSHIP

Become a leader who others love to follow.

Be willing to step past fear and set aside ego for the greater goal of creating something awesome alongside your team.

Be just as comfortable supporting as you are leading. View your team with a perspective based in truth and carry an attitude of alignment that assumes the best rather than assumes the worst.

Make your people your most important resource. Rather than bend over backwards to create one amazing performance, care for yourself and for your team so that together you can consistently perform amazingly.

When you lead, be bold, specific, and, above all authentic. True to the mission, true to your team and true to yourself.

You've got this.

Now act.

About the Author

Andrew Bright owns and acts with <u>The Panic Squad Improv Comedy</u>. He has been a professional comedian with The Panic Squad for over twenty years and has had the  privilege of performing across the United States and Canada for diverse events ranging from local churches and businesses to large national conferences and top Fortune 500 corporations. Live audiences have ranged from the 6 people who attended his first public show in 1996, to over 35,000.

Understanding how to lead and function within a team is essential to succeeding in improv. Out of his combined passion for improv comedy and leadership, Andrew created a number of professional development workshops that use improv comedy to teach key elements of teamwork, leadership, and stage presentation. His workshops have been creating change in organizations across North America.

When not performing, teaching or speaking, Andrew does his most challenging and cherished work. Taking the lead role as husband to his wife, Karla, and father to four energetic young children. Talk about improv! The Brights make their home in beautiful Northwest Washington State.

Connect with Andrew:

Blog: www.andrewbright.me
Facebook: /AndrewBrightOfficial
Twitter: @AndrewIsBright
Instagram: @PanicAndrew

Connect with The Panic Squad Improv Comedy:

Website: www.panicsquad.com
Facebook: /thepanicsquad
Twitter: @panicsquad

Notes

[1] Pat's POV "An Unconventional Gift" – December 2011 - http://hosted-p0.vresp.com/305805/42037a5094/ARCHIVE

[2] Ibid

[3] New Oxford American Dictionary- 2015 Apple Inc. – Version 2.2.1

[4] The Bible – New International Version

[5] Ibid

[6] *Bad Ink* – Television Show (A&E Network)

[7] NewYork Times – February 3rd – 2014 - http://www.nytimes.com/2014/02/03/sports/football/russell-wilson-the-forgotten-quarterback-coolly-orchestrates-a-perfect-football-game.html?_r=3

[8] Jon Acuff, Do Over – Rescue Monday, Reinvent You Work, and Never Get Stuck (Portfolio/Penguin USA 2015) Page 213

[9] Ibid – Front Cover

[10] Carey Nieuwhof, Impact – 7 Powerful Conversations That Will Help Your Church Grow (The reThink Group, Inc. USA 2015) Page 101

11 Ibid – Page 102

12 Eric Samuel Timm – Orator, Author, Artist, Visionary—Battling The Darkness By Broadcasting Truth Experientially And Multidimensionally, http://ericsamueltimm.com

13 *The Price is Right*, CBS Network, FremantleMedia

14 *The Price is Right*, CBS, FremantleMedia, Season 43 – Episode 150

15 Carey Nieuwhof, *The Carey Nieuwhof Leadership Podcast*, Episode 64

16 Jon Acuff – 30 Days of Hustle Challenge - http://acuff.me/30dohchallenge

17 Andrew Bright - *Life, Leadership and Teamwork Through The Lens Of Improv Comedy*, http://www.andrewbright.me

18 Bloodhounds   - https://en.wikipedia.org/wiki/Bloodhound

19 *Hitch*, Directed by Andy Tennant (USA Columbia Pictures 2005) DVD

20 *The Lord of The Rings - The Two Towers*, Directed by Peter Jackson, (USA, Newline Cinema 2002) DVD

[21] *Frozen*, Directed by Chris Buck and Jennifer Lee (USA Walt Disney Animation Studios/Walt Disney Pictures, 2013) DVD

[22] Carey Nieuwhof, Impact – 7 Powerful Conversations That Will Help Your Church Grow (The reThink Group, Inc. USA 2015) Pages 103-104

[23] The Panic Squad Improv Comedy, Successful Missions, http://www.panicsquad.com/successful-missions/

[24] The Panic Squad Improv Comedy, Failed Missions, http://www.panicsquad.com/failed-missions/

[25] Patrick Lencioni, *The Advantage – Why Organizational Health Trumps Everything Else in Business* (Jossy-Bass USA 2012) Page 27

[26] Ibid

[27] Ibid